EXPLORING THE ROOTS OF 15 CURRENT GLOBAL ISSUES

国際問題のルーツを探る

石谷由美子

NAN'UN-DO

Download Audio

音声ファイル
無料 DL
のご案内

このテキストの音声を無料で視聴（ストリーミング）・ダウンロードできます。自習用音声としてご活用ください。
以下のサイトにアクセスしてテキスト番号で検索してください。

https://nanun-do.com　テキスト番号［**512213**］

※ 無線 LAN（WiFi）に接続してのご利用を推奨いたします。

※ 音声ダウンロードは Zip ファイルでの提供になります。
お使いの機器によっては別途ソフトウェア（アプリケーション）の導入が必要となります。

※ Exploring the Roots of 15 Current Global Issues
音声ダウンロードページは以下の QR コードからもご利用になれます。

Read by

Emma Howard
Michael Rhys

Exploring the Roots of 15 Current Global Issues

● 本書が目標としているもの

2022年は日本のみならず世界にとっても大きな転換点を迎えた年と言えます。ロシアがウクライナに侵攻し、中国が香港や台湾に圧力をかけたことで、様々な問題が浮き彫りになりました。国連が機能しないことで国連のあり方に疑問が生じ、NATOなど集団防衛を考えざるをえず、平和主義・非核を訴えていた日本も現実問題としてそれが難しくなっていることを認識してきています。もちろん全世界に広まったコロナの問題も見逃せません。平和主義を掲げる日本にとってこうした状況で重要なことは、いかに早く国際問題の本質、そしてその行方を読み解くことです。本書は、現在起きている多くの国際問題を理解することを目標として作成されています。英字新聞や英語雑誌を幅広く読み、また問題を英語で説明する、話す、議論する、まで持っていくための礎石となることを目指しています。国際問題を読み解く際に本書が骨格としているものが、その問題のルーツから読み解こうというものです。今起きている国際問題は昨日・今日勃発したものではなく、長い間かかって、いわゆる「熟成」したものであることがわかります。ロシアがウクライナに侵攻した時にも、日本人の多くは「なぜ？」と考えたと思います。中国と香港・台湾の関係も100年、200年の蓄積から現在の状態に至っています。これまでの経緯に注意を払っておけばそれぞれの問題が「なるべくして起こった」と解釈されることが多々あります。これからどこで何が起こるか？それを事前に阻止する方法はないか？など、我々は常に神経を尖らせておかなければなりません。特に「軍隊」を持たない我々ができることはこうした情報収集能力になります。インターネットが発達している現在、世界の人がどのように考えているのか、我々が知らないどういう情報があるのかを知るのに英語の読み書き能力は当然必要になってきます。本書は英語でのさらなる上の情報を読み解く「つなぎ」となることができれば、と考えております。

本書で目標にしているのは要約すると次の3点です。

1. 国際問題を歴史や民族の問題を含めてルーツから見ていくこと。
2. 必要な専門用語と基礎知識を身につけて、英字新聞や国際放送、インターネット情報にアクセスする力をつける。
3. 簡単な構文を使ってニュースを英語でsummarizeする力を身につける。

実際にニュース英語はいかに素早く誤解のないようにものごとを伝えるかを目指しているので、構文的には読者を惑わせようとするものではありません。難しいのはその背景を知っているか、専門用語を知っているか、その発音を知っているかにかかっています。本書をステップにして英語で国際問題を読み、語る学生が増えてくれることを期待しております。最後に、南雲堂のJim Knudsen氏が英文のチェックをしてくださいました。根気よく見てくださり感謝いたします。またChristofer Bullsmith氏にも協力をいただきました。

石谷由美子

● 本書の構成

左頁	右頁
	① カバーページ
② 本文	③ 本文
④ 問題（日本語）	⑤ 問題（英語）
⑥ Episode 1	⑦ 問題（英語）
⑧ Episode 2　問題（英語）	

本書は各課上記のように８ページによって構成されています。②と③の本文はまとめて一つですので、全体が見渡せるように見開きにしています。

P.1: カバーページ：その課のトピックに合わせたwarming up用のクイズを付しておきました。課を読んでから最後にこのクイズに戻ってきてもいいでしょう。トピックの場所の位置を確認するために地図を配しています。

P.2 & 3: 本文：それぞれのトピックについて基本は「概観→民族・言語・宗教→歴史→現在の状況」、という構成です。専門用語も出てきますが、すぐに参照できるように、右ページの下にNotesをつけておきました。構文的には難しいものではないので、一気に読んで歴史の流れと内容を把握してください。

P.4 & 5:「本文」に関する問題。P.4で、(1) 日本語での内容確認。本文で読んだ内容が掴めているかを確認します。P.5の方は、(2) 年表の空欄を埋めて歴史の流れを掴む。(3) True or False問題。英語で内容を確認します。

P.6 & 7: Episode1―それぞれのトピックについて「関連した話題」を簡単に載せてあります。こちらの方はさっと読んで、簡単な英語の問題に答えてください。

P.8 : Epidode2―Episode 1よりも短い内容のエピソードを載せてあります。簡単に英語の質問を付してあります。（エピソードは３つある課もあります）

● その他の注意

1. 本書で扱っている国際問題は2023年10月現在の状況です。国際問題は刻一刻と変化しているので、このテキストを読み進めている時にも新しい変化･進展が考えられます。
2. 国名の表示
   Russiaは、1917-1991の間のものについては、Soviet Unionを使用しています。UKは、1603年までもしくはScotlandとの対比を表す時にはEngland、1603年にEnglandとScotlandが一つになってからはBritain、そしてUnited Kingdom of Great Britain and Irelandの成立の1801年以降はUKを使用しています。(区別がはっきりしないところもありますが)。またウクライナのKievはKyivにしてありますがKievan-Rus'（キエフ・ロシア）は、歴史書ではKievanを使ってあるのでそのままにしてあります。

Contents

Unit
1

Ukraine
The Russian invasion of Ukraine

1. How much do you know about Ukraine?
2. How much do you know about Crimea?
3. What led Russia to invade Ukraine in 2022?
4. What was the name of Ukraine's president in 2022?

1 **Outline** In the 18th century, Ukraine, then an independent country, fell under Russian rule. The country regained its independence in 1991 when the Soviet Union broke up. However, Russia has been constantly intervening in Ukraine's affairs, because Ukraine is economically, geographically, and militarily vital to today's Russia. The current situation is that when Ukraine became free in 1991, it began seeking closer ties to the West. Russia, feeling threatened, intervened in Ukraine and annexed Crimea. Russia then urged Donetsk and Luhansk, eastern provinces of Ukraine, to gain their independence from Ukraine. Then, in 2022, Russia launched an all-out attack on Ukraine.

2 **Ethnicity, language and religion** Ukrainians, Belarusians, and Russians all belong to the East Slavic ethnic group that is native to Ukraine. Their languages are closely related, since they all have the same linguistic root; the East Slavic subgroup of Slavic languages. In many respects, these three peoples have shared the same history. They all once belonged to Kievan Rus' (now Ukraine). As for religion, by the 10th century, Kievan Rus' had fallen under the influence of the Byzantine Empire and had converted to Orthodox Christianity. According to a 2019 survey, 82% of Ukrainians were Christians, of which 72.9% called themselves Orthodox Christians.

3 **History** You might be surprised to learn that Russia grew out of Ukraine. The place known as Ukraine actually came into being first. Ukraine was much more powerful and prosperous than Russia, and a civilized country influenced by western ideas and culture. Russia, on the other hand, was a backward region far to the east. Kievan Rus' kingdom was founded by Germanic Vikings from Scandinavia, who conquered the local Slavic tribes and mixed with them. Kyiv was the center of a powerful Kievan Rus' Kingdom, which in the 9th century reached all the way from the Baltic Sea to the Black Sea. In the 10th century, they accepted Orthodox Christianity. In the 13th century, Mongols invaded Kyiv, and power shifted north to Moscow, which at that time was just a small trading city. It was through this Mongolian invasion of Kievan Rus' that the power positions of Russia and Ukraine switched. Russia became a powerful Russian state. Ukraine, meanwhile, was dominated by Lithuania, and then by the Polish-Lithuanian Commonwealth.

4 **Ukraine under Russian rule** In the mid-17th century, Ukraine gradually came under the rule of the Russian Empire and, in the 18th century, became a part of Russia. When the Russian Empire collapsed during WWI, Ukraine became an independent state (1917). But not for long: it was soon incorporated into the newly formed Soviet Union in 1922. Ukrainian peasants resisted the Soviets, but Stalin oppressed them and started a man-made famine (1932-1933) called Holodomor (hunger-extermination, or "The Great Famine"), which killed millions of Ukrainian people. Stalin then replaced Ukrainians with millions of Russians, who farmed the eastern part of Ukraine. This mass migration weakened

Ukrainian nationalism in the east.

5 **WWII** When the Nazis invaded Ukraine in 1941 during WWII, some Ukrainians welcomed them as liberators. However, the Nazis betrayed Ukrainians' expectations and began a brutal campaign against them. Toward the end of the War, many Ukrainians were fighting against the Nazis and Stalin's Red Army at the same time. In the end, Ukraine became one of the world's bloodiest battlefields. Some 6 million Ukrainians died during the war, including an estimated 1.5 million Jews.

6 **Independence** In 1991, when the Soviet Union dissolved and fell, Ukraine declared its independence. The country's biggest trading partner was still Russia, but Ukraine started leaning toward the EU and NATO, a movement that worried Russia and eventually led to the Russo-Ukrainian War of 2014.

7 **Ukrainian Revolution and the Russo-Ukrainian War (2014)** Yanukovych, Ukraine's president (2010-2014), adopted pro-Russian policies, which irritated and angered many Ukrainians. He was forced to flee to Russia in February 2014, an event that is called the "Ukrainian Revolution" or the "Maidan Revolution." Responding to this, Russia invaded the Crimean Peninsula and formally annexed it in March 2014. In April, pro-Russian groups in the eastern part of Ukraine rebelled against the Ukrainian government, with Donetsk and Luhansk declaring their independence from Ukraine. In August, to support these areas, Russian military vehicles crossed the border into the region. To end this conflict, Russia, Donetsk, and Luhansk all signed an agreement with Ukraine in Minsk on 5 September 2014 (the Minsk Protocol). Donetsk and Luhansk declared their independence, but the UN did not recognize them as states. This period is called the Russo-Ukrainian War. Many countries criticized Russian actions, but in 2022, finally, Russia invaded Ukraine.

Notes

1 intervene 干渉する　vital 重要な　threaten 脅かす　annex 併合する　urge A toV「A に V させる」 launch 始める　all-out 全面的な

2 be native to ～ ～生まれである　subgroup サブグループ（亜種）　Kievan Rus' キエフ・ロシア（キエフ大公国）　the Byzantine Empire ビザンツ帝国　convert 改宗する　the Orthodox 正教会

3 prosperous 繁栄した　backward（文化などの）遅れた　Germanic Vikings ゲルマン系バイキング　shift 移動する　switch 交替する　dominate 支配する

4 incorporate 組み込む　peasant 農民　oppress 抑圧する　a man-made famine 恣意的な飢饉　hunger-extermination 飢餓による民族絶滅　replace A with B：A を B に置き換える　farm 耕す　migration 移民

5 liberator 解放者　betray 裏切る　brutal 残酷な　Red Army 赤軍　bloody 流血の　battlefield 戦場

6 dissolve 解体する　lean toward ～ ～へ傾く

7 irritate イライラさせる　anger 怒らせる　flee-fled-fled 逃げる　rebel 反乱する　vehicle 車両　the Minsk Protocol ミンスク合意

【1】次の質問に日本語で答えよ。

1 1991年のウクライナ独立後もロシアがウクライナに干渉し続ける理由は？

2 ロシア人、ウクライナ人、ベラルーシ人はかつて一つの国であったが、その国とは？

3 ロシアとウクライナの立場が代わったのは何が原因か？

4 ウクライナの東部でウクライナのナショナリズムが弱いのはなぜか？

5 第二次世界大戦中のウクライナ人のナチスへの対応はどうであったか？

6 1991年、ロシアからの独立後、ウクライナはどういう政策をとったか？

7 2014年にロシアがウクライナ東部に侵入したのはどういう理由からか？

【2】Complete the following timetable in English

9C	Kievan Rus became powerful
10C	Kievan Rus converted to Eastern Orthodox Christianity.
13C	Mongols invaded. → power shifted to ([1])
18C	Ukraine became a part of the ([2]) Empire.
1917-1922	Ukraine gained independence (1917). → incorporated in the Soviet Union(1922).
1932	Holodomor (=the Great ([3]))
WWII	Ukraine was one of the bloodiest battlefields.
1991	Ukraine declared its independence.
2014	Ukrainian Revolution → Russia occupied ([4]) and declared independence of ([5]) and Luhansk. → Russia invaded Ukraine (the Russo-Ukrainian War) → Minsk Protocol

【3】True or False

1) Russian civilization grew out of Moscow. ( )

2) Kievan Rus' was founded by Germanic Vikings. ( )

3) Mongols invaded Kievan Rus, which affected the history of Ukraine and Russia. ( )

4) When the Russian Empire collapsed during WWI, Ukraine gained its independence for a short time. ( )

5) The Great Famine of 1932-1933 was man-made. ( )

6) After the Holodomor famine, Stalin encouraged many Russians to live in the eastern part of Ukraine. ( )

7) As the result of immigration from Russia, Ukrainian nationalism in the east weakened. ( )

8) During WWII, some Ukrainians at first welcomed the Nazis, hoping that they would liberate Ukraine. ( )

9) In response to the Ukrainian Revolution in 2014, Russia occupied Crimea. ( )

10) The UN admitted Donetsk and Luhansk as independent states. ( )

Episode 1 **Russian invasion of Ukraine (2022)**

On 21st February 2022, Russia declared the independence of Donetsk and Luhansk. On the 24th, just after the Winter Beijing Olympic Games closed, Russia invaded Ukraine. The invasion received widespread international criticism.

Putin, the Russian president, stated that his primary aim was to protect the people living in these regions. His real aim, however, was to stop the expansion of NATO, a western military alliance. The old Warsaw Pact for the communist eastern-bloc countries had disappeared with the collapse of the Soviet Union in 1991, and many Eastern European countries had already joined NATO. Ukraine was also approaching NATO, but Putin didn't want NATO's further expansion and he wanted to replace Ukraine's pro-NATO government led by Zelensky with a pro-Russian government.

Russia's invasion of Ukraine was also criticised by the UN, but Western countries were prevented from sending troops to help the Ukrainians directly, because Ukraine was not yet a NATO member. The UN couldn't do anything, either, because some countries like China and India rejected any such action. The US also hesitated because their action might encourage Russia to use nuclear arms. Many people around the world thought that Ukraine would surrender immediately, but the Ukrainian fighters, led by President Zelensky, persistently resisted.

Instead of sending troops, many countries resorted to economic sanctions and some provided Ukraine with arms. This war showed the power of a new weapon: the Internet and drones. Zelensky and many Ukrainians made use of SNS, uploading pictures and movies of bombings and damaged buildings. In "traditional" wars, TV was used, but TV news was likely to be distorted by some government power or authority. But the Internet messages and videos sent by local people directly appealed to the world. It is said that the US and some other countries secretly assisted Ukraine by using their new technology to give accurate information about Russian military movements.

1. Putin justified their invasion of Ukraine, saying …
   (1) Ukraine joined NATO.
   (2) Ukraine became increasingly being militarised.
   (3) Ukraine became hostile to Russia.
   (4) his aim was to protect the people there.

2. Putin's real intention was …
   (1) to prevent Ukraine from joining NATO.
   (2) to join NATO
   (3) to build a stronger military organization than NATO.
   (4) to rule Europe.

3. Western countries could not send troops to help Ukraine, because …
   (1) Ukraine was partly to blame for the war.
   (2) Ukraine was not yet a NATO member.
   (3) they thought that Ukraine would be immediately defeated.
   (4) they thought economic sanctions would be enough to defeat Russia.

4. What new weapon was used in this war?
   (1) land mines (2) tanks (3) the Internet (4) volunteer soldiers

NATO's expansion since 1997

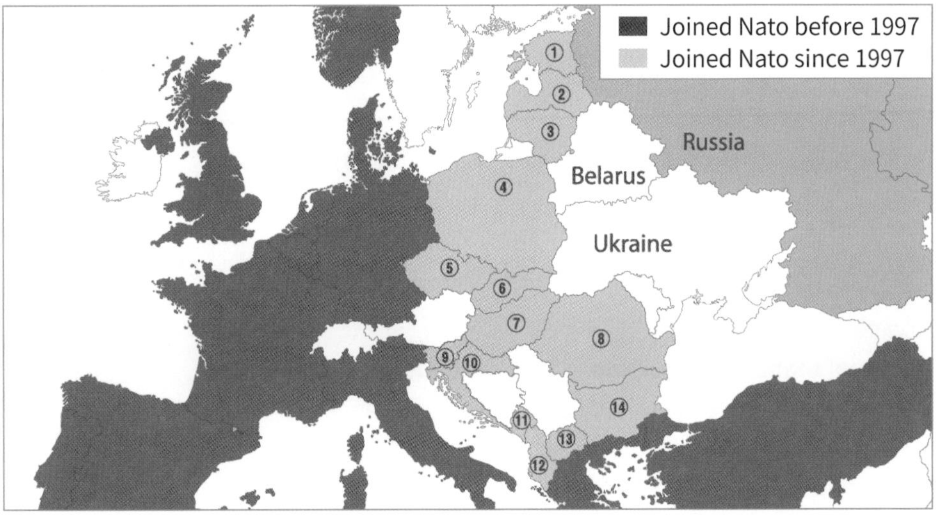

① Estonia
② Latvia
③ Lithuania
④ Poland
⑤ Czech Republic
⑥ Slovakia
⑦ Hungary
⑧ Romania
⑨ Slovenia
⑩ Croatia
⑪ Montenegro
⑫ Albania
⑬ North Macedonia
⑭ Bulgaria

＊ Sweden and Finland joined in 2023

Notes

military alliance 軍事同盟　the Warsaw Pact ワルシャワ条約機構　surrender 降伏する　persistently ねばり強く　resort to ～に訴える　economic sanction 経済制裁　upload アップロードする　distort 歪曲する　accurate 正確な

Episode 2 Volodymyr Zelensky (Ukrainian president at war)

Zelensky was born to Jewish parents in 1978 in Ukraine. His father was a professor in computer science, and his mother was an engineer. Zelensky got a degree in law at the Kiev National Economic University. He then entered the world of comedy and appeared in a popular TV show, "Servant of the People," which ran from 2015 to 2019. In the show, Zelensky played the role of Ukrainian president. But then, Zelensky actually stood for president in the 2019 Ukrainian election, and won. Called a populist, he was an anti-establishment, anti-corruption figure who made effective use of social media. When Russia invaded Ukraine in 2022, Zelensky stayed in Kyiv and fought against the Russian army, appealing to the world through the Internet the righteousness of his and his country's struggle. Putin, meanwhile, justified his actions, claiming that Zelensky was involved in atrocities against Russians in Ukraine. Whether Putin's claim was true or not, Zelensky and his country received sympathy from many countries. Although Russia was obviously a stronger military power than Ukraine, and although many people thought that Ukraine soon would surrender, Ukraine persistently fought the Russians. Zelensky used his communication skills and accurate information and weapons provided by western countries.

1. Zelensky's parents are …
   (1) Ukrainian (2) Jewish (3) Russian (4) unknown

2. Zelensky studied … at university.
   (1) economics (2) comedy (3) law (4) literature

3. "Servant of the People" is …
   (1) a novel that Zelensky wrote.
   (2) a play in which Zelensky played a military general.
   (3) an economic organization.
   (4) a TV drama in which Zelensky played the role of president.

4. Zelensky was …
   (1) a conservative president. (2) a progressive president.
   (3) a comical president. (4) a communist president.

Notes

Jewish ユダヤ人の degree 学位 run 続く stand for 立候補する populist 大衆主義者 anti-establishment 反体制 anti-corruption 反腐敗 figure 人物 righteousness 正義 justify 正当化する atrocity 虐殺 sympathy 同情 surrender 降伏する persistently 粘り強く

Unit

2

Ireland

"The Troubles" in Northern Ireland

1. What is the capital city of Ireland?

2. What is the full name of the UK?

3. What is the main religion of Ireland?

4. What is the main religion of the UK?

5. What are two main religions of Northern Ireland?

1 **Outline** Ireland is an island off the western coast of England. The island is divided, with the southern half as an independent nation and the northern half, known as Northern Ireland, a part of the UK. Originally, it was one country, but history changed the fate of the country. In the latter part of the 20th century, a terrorist group carried out violent acts: the Irish Republican Army, or IRA, of Northern Ireland. The group's goal was to reunite Ireland. Northern Ireland has long had a dilemma. It is geographically part of Ireland, while politically and religiously, it has been part of the UK for many centuries. That's because starting in the 16th century, England began invading the northern part of the Irish island and began sending Protestant people to live in the area. What this means is that, today, there are many Protestants in Northern Ireland. For a long time, Ireland demanded that Northern Ireland should be returned to Ireland. The UK always refused, which led to many violent conflicts and many acts of terrorism (by the IRA). But in 1998, the Good Friday Agreement was finally reached, and the Northern Ireland's "dilemma" seemed settled. But in January 2020, the UK left the European Union (EU), and this problem has once again arisen.

2 **Ethnicity, language and religion** History says that about 500 BC, Ireland was settled by a group of people called the Celts who came from mainland Europe. They spoke Gaelic, a language that is still spoken by some Irish people, although the official language of Ireland is English. Irish people were originally pagan, meaning non-Christian, but in the early fifth century, a Roman missionary named St. Patrick came to Ireland and spread Christianity. Christian monks also brought the Roman alphabet to Ireland with them. In the ninth century, Vikings came from Scandinavia and settled in Ireland, mixing with the Celts, which formed the basis of the Irish people.

3 **English Rule over Ireland** In 1066, England was conquered by a group called the Normans from France (the Norman Conquest). By around the 12th century, they had moved into Ireland, and such Norman and English rule over Ireland continued for several centuries. In the 16th century, the Reformation, when England became Protestant, brought hardship to the Irish people because they remained Catholic. Henry VIII started military campaigns against Ireland, and many Irish people were killed. He also started a "plantation" policy. This meant that land was taken away from Catholic Irish landowners and given to Protestant settlers from England and Scotland. In this way, England populated northern Ireland with more and more Protestants. In the 17th century, at last, Ireland was conquered by the British and many laws were passed that discriminated against Catholics. The native Irish Gaelic language was banned from being taught in schools. In 1800, the Irish Parliament was abolished, and Ireland became part of "the United Kingdom of Great Britain and Ireland." But Catholics were not allowed to be members of parliament (MPs) until 1829.

4 **The Independence of Ireland and "The Troubles"** In 1845, a terrible potato famine struck Ireland. Many Irish people died or fled to other countries. Ireland lost 20-25% of its population, and 10-20% of the Irish people left the country in the years following the great famine. During this time, England did nothing to help the Irish people, while at the same time they exploited Irish farmers. This angered the Irish people and led to a movement to secure Ireland's autonomy (Home Rule). A huge anti-British riot took place on Easter Day (1916), but it was put down and its leaders were arrested and punished. Such brutal treatment by England led to an even stronger movement for independence on the Irish side. The Irish War of Independence broke out in 1919 and continued until 1921. In 1922, the southern 26 counties of Ireland became independent from the UK. The other six counties in the north of Ireland remained part of the UK, and still are part of it as Northern Ireland. The new country of the southern part was called "the Irish Free State." Gaelic was restored as their official language, along with English. In 1948, Ireland became officially called "the Republic of Ireland." The name "Eire" was used from 1937 as an official name for the independent country of Ireland. "Eire" is an Irish word meaning "love," but since the 1998 Good Friday Agreement, "Ireland" has been used as the country's official name. "Ireland" is an English word that means "Eire's land." All these historical conflicts over Northern Ireland between Ireland and the UK are known collectively as "The Troubles."

Notes

1 the Irish Republican Army アイルランド共和軍　dilemma ジレンマ　Good Friday Agreement ベルファスト合意 settle 決着させる　arise-arose-arisen 起き上がる

2 Celts ケルト人　Gaelic ゲール語　pagan 異教徒　missionary 宣教師

3 Reformation 宗教改革　plantation 植民　populate A with B　A に B を殖民させる　discriminate 差別する　ban 禁止する　parliament 議会　abolish 廃止する　MP (Member of Parliament) 議員

4 famine 飢饉　flee-fled-fled 逃げる　exploit 搾取する　anger 怒らせる　autonomy 自治　riot 暴動　be put down 鎮静化される　arrest 逮捕する　punish 罰する　county 州　restore 復活させる　collectively まとめて

【1】次の質問に日本語で答えよ。

1 IRAとはどういう組織か？　彼らの目的は？

2 アイルランド人を民族的に説明せよ。

3 ヘンリー8世の宗教改革がアイルランドにもたらした影響とは？

4 1) アイルランド人が自治（Home Rule）を求めるきっかけとなったのは何か？

2) 1919-1921年のアイルランド独立運動はどういう結果になったか？

3) 1960年代後半から1998年までの約30年間に渡る北アイルランドでの紛争はどう呼ばれているか？

【2】Complete the following timetable in English

500BC	([1]) came to Ireland.
5C	St. ([2]) introduced Christianity.
1066	Norman Conquest
16C	The Reformation by Henry VIII in England, but ([3]) remained Catholic. → England started military campaigns against Irish people. → Land: Catholic Irish landowners → Protestant settlers from England and Scotland
17C	Ireland was conquered by England.
1845	([4]) Famine → Many Irish people died.
1922	The southern part of Ireland = The Irish Free State The northern part of Ireland = part of the UK (Northern Ireland)
1998	"Ireland" ← the Good ([5]) Agreement

【3】True or False

1) The IRA was a group aiming to reunite Ireland and England. ( )

2) England used to be Catholic, but it converted to the Protestant religion in the 16th century. ( )

3) The aim of the British invasion of Northern Ireland was to populate the area with British Protestants. ( )

4) The first people to settle in Ireland were the Vikings. ( )

5) The Roman missionary St. Patrick introduced Christianity to the Irish. ( )

6) The policy known as "Plantation" meant that England encouraged Protestant British people to replace Catholic landowners in Ireland. ( )

7) In 1800, Ireland was incorporated into the UK under the name of "the United Kingdom of Great Britain and Ireland". ( )

8) "Home Rule" referred to the Irish people's desire to make Ireland a free, independent state. ( )

9) In 1922, the whole of Ireland gained independence from the UK. ( )

10) Ireland used to be called "Eire," but after the 1988 Good Friday Agreement, "Ireland" became the country's official name, because "Ireland" was a word from Gaelic, the people's native language. ( )

Episode 1 Reformation: the religious split of England and Ireland

In the 16th century, King Henry VIII of England had a big problem. He wanted to divorce his Spanish wife Catherine because she had not been able to give birth to a son, only to a daughter named Mary. Henry wanted a boy badly, a son who would become his heir. But there was another reason that Henry wanted to divorce Catherine. He had fallen in love with a court lady, Anne Boleyn, and wanted to marry her. But that was not possible. Both Henry and Catherine were Catholic, and according to the laws of the Catholic Church, divorce was not permitted. So what did Henry do? He converted to the Protestant religion, which did permit divorce. He established his own Protestant faith, the Anglican Church, with himself as its head. In the end, Henry divorced Catherine and married Anne. However, Anne gave him no son either—only another daughter, Elizabeth. Henry married six women in total. He got a boy from one of those wives, Jane Seymour. That son was Edward VI, but he died young. With no male successors available, Henry's daughter Mary became queen. But she died young, too, and Elizabeth became queen. She reigned for a long time, but died childless, so the English throne went to the only male available, Henry VIII's sister's great-grandson James VI. He was then the King of Scotland, but he became King of England as James I, and ruled both Scotland and England, unifying the two countries. James, by the way, was Catholic, but to rule England, he accepted the Protestant Anglican Church of England. It was in this way that England and Scotland became a Protestant country, and Ireland remained Catholic.

King Henry VIII and his six wives

1. Why did Henry VIII want to divorce his first wife, Catherine?
   (1) She was Catholic.
   (2) She was Spanish.
   (3) She couldn't give him a son.
   (4) She wasn't Catholic.

2. Why couldn't Henry VIII divorce Catherine?
   (1) She had a daughter.
   (2) She didn't want to return to Spain.
   (3) Henry was Catholic.
   (4) Catherine was only a court lady.

3. What solution to this problem did Henry choose?
   (1) He talked to the Pope in Rome.
   (2) He gave up the throne.
   (3) He adopted a son.
   (4) He established his own church.

4. The Anglican Church is…
   (1) Catholic (2) Scottish (3) Orthodox (4) Protestant

5. How did James VI of Scotland become King of England?
   (1) He was adopted by Elizabeth I.
   (2) He converted to Catholicism.
   (3) He was Elizabeth I's closest male relative.
   (4) He was Edward VI's grandson.

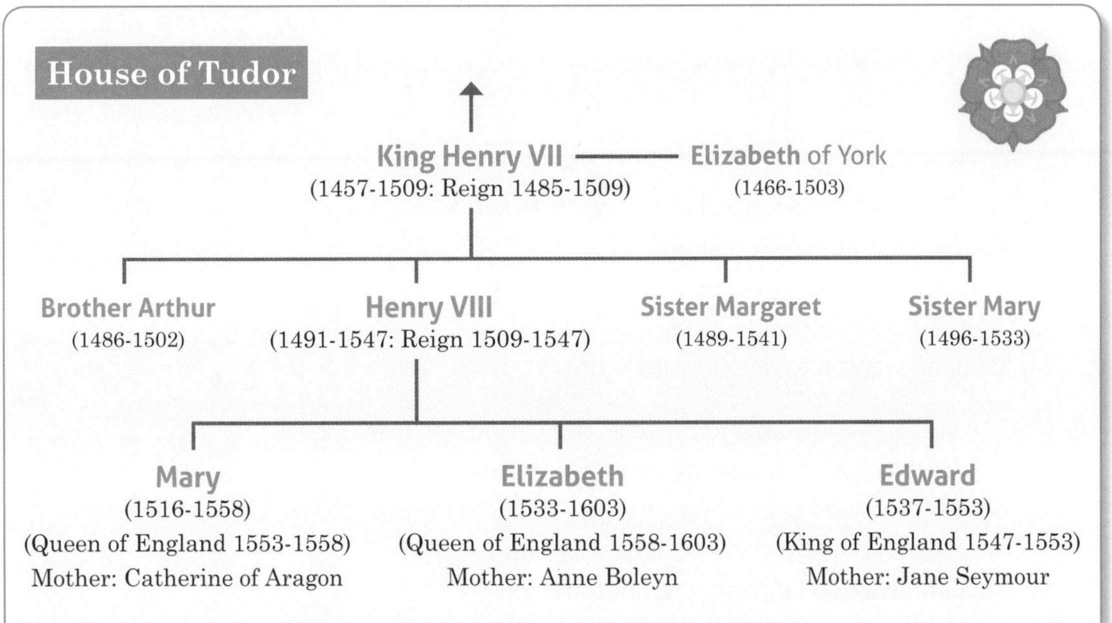

参照 https://www.henryviiithereign.co.uk/henry-viiis-family-tree-including-siblings.html

Notes

Reformation 宗教改革 split 分裂 heir 後継者 a court lady 女官 convert 改宗する in quest for ～を求めて successor 後継者 available 得られる reign 統治する throne 王座 unify 統合する

Episode 2 **Prospect of Scottish independence**

When Elizabeth I died in 1603, the next king was James I, who, at the same time, was James VI of Scotland. James unified Scotland and England. This didn't mean, however, that both countries were completely united into one nation. They were still two politically separate kingdoms, each with its own parliament. In 1707, England and Scotland were unified as "Great Britain" under Queen Anne. There were several reasons for this union. First, Scotland realized they needed strong support from England to build colonies overseas. Second, many Scots were afraid of the restoration of the Stuarts, a Catholic Royal family. As for England, the country feared that Scotland might cooperate with France, England's enemy. This partly unified state has continued for three centuries. But since WWII, there has been an increase in nationalism in Wales, Scotland, and Northern Ireland. Scotland held a national referendum over independence in 2014; 55% of Scottish voters rejected leaving the UK. However, in the 2016 EU membership referendum, Scotland and Northern Ireland voted to remain in the EU, while England and Wales voted to leave. In fact, in 2020 the UK did leave the EU. In response, there is now a movement against this decision from the Scottish side. It is likely that someday soon, there will be a second Scottish independence referendum.

1. In 1603, England and Scotland were united. How?
   (1) England conquered Scotland.
   (2) The Scottish king succeeded to the English throne.
   (3) James (I or VI) became Catholic.
   (4) England wanted to reunite with Scotland.

2. In 1707, England and Scotland became one nation because…
   (1) England needed Scotland for economic reasons.
   (2) Scotland needed strong support from England to compete with other countries.
   (3) England wanted Scotland to become Protestant.
   (4) Scotland wanted England's technology.

3. Now, Scotland is thinking of leaving the UK. Why?
   (1) The UK left the EU.
   (2) Scotland wants to join Ireland.
   (3) The UK does not need Scotland any more.
   (4) Scotland wants its own parliament.

Notes

prospect 見込み　unify 統一する　restoration 復活　the Stuarts スチュアート朝　referendum 国民投票

Unit
3

Brexit

Why did the UK leave the EU?

1. Can you name the six original member countries of the EU, or European Union?

2. What does "Brexit" mean or refer to?

3. Why did the UK decide to leave the EU?

1 **Outline** The United Kingdom (UK) formally left the EU on 31 January 2020. This departure has been called "Brexit," an abbreviation of "British Exit." A referendum was held in the UK in 2016 to decide whether the country should remain in or leave the EU. When the votes were counted, 52% of the people voted "Leave" while 48% voted "Remain." Although the results were close enough to raise some doubt and debate, the UK ultimately decided to get out of the EU. What made the UK and the British people come to this decision? Several factors came into play. Many years before, when the idea of "European unification" first came up, the UK was reluctant to join. At the time, the UK believed that it didn't need to join such a body because it had a strong political and economic relationship with the United States and the former British Commonwealth. Even after the UK joined the EU, in some ways it remained independent. For example, it kept its own currency—the British pound—and still required visitors from EU countries to show their passports when they entered the country. Thus, it was not really all that surprising that the UK voted to leave.

2 **The history of EU and its expansion** Six countries (France, Italy, Luxembourg, the Netherlands, Belgium, and West Germany) established the European Coal and Steel Community (ECSC) in 1951. These six original member countries are called the "Inner Six." The ECSC became the European Economic Community (EEC) in 1957, and then the European Community (EC) in 1967. In 1960, responding to the "Inner Six," seven other countries in Europe formed the European Free Trade Association (EFTA). These seven members (the UK, Denmark, Ireland, Norway, Sweden, Austria, and Switzerland) became known as the "Outer Seven." However, the UK started to realize that cooperation with the EEC would be necessary. The UK, along with Denmark, Ireland, and Norway, applied for membership in 1961. But French President Charles de Gaulle, thinking that Britain's participation might cause problems, rejected their applications. They tried again in 1967, and this time they were accepted by the new French President Pompidou. In 1973, the UK, Denmark, and Ireland officially joined the EC. In 1981, Greece also joined and in 1986, Portugal joined along with Spain. Sweden, Austria, and Finland soon followed. The EC became the EU (European Union) in 1993, with the number of EU members reaching 28. After Brexit, the EU has 27 members (2020). Switzerland has always remained outside the EU.

3 **Why did UK decide to leave the EU?** Three basic reasons can be pointed out.

1. Sovereignty

One reason commonly cited for Brexit was that the British wanted to protect their "sovereignty." In other words, they wanted to deal with their political, economic, and judicial matters by themselves. They wanted to make and sell products and food freely in the way that was most suitable for them. They also wanted a court system and an education system that upheld their own values. The British, having been a proud, independent nation for a very long time, didn't like EU's restrictions.

2. Immigrants

Before the Brexit referendum, there had been a considerable increase in the number of immigrants coming into the UK from EU countries. In 2014, that number was 268,000, up from 201,000 in 2013. According to *The Economist*, 94% of geographical areas that had seen an increase of over 200% in their foreign-born population between 2001 and 2014 supported "Leave." Such immigrants were seen as taking many British people's jobs. Anger built up among "native" Brits, who felt that their tax money should be used to support British people, not immigrants.

3. Economy

Inequality was becoming greater and greater in terms of the economic burden each EU member should bear. Inside the EU, richer countries are required to help poorer countries. To maintain the EU, member countries must contribute a certain amount of money, usually calculated according to each country's economic power. The UK was the second largest economic power after Germany in the EU. This meant that it paid 10% of the EU budget. That money went to poorer countries, not to the UK. Because the UK had then many economic problems of its own, many people were of the opinion that more money should be used for the UK.

4 **The result** As the result of Brexit, the EU lost its second-largest economy, its third-most populous country, and the second-largest contributor to the EU budget (in 2016, Germany paid 14.5 billion euros, the UK paid 11.5 billion euros, and France paid 5.5 billion euros). But the UK has also suffered. Many businesses soon left the UK, which was a big blow to the UK economy. The British will have to wait for several more years to know whether Brexit was or was not the right decision for them.

Notes

1 abbreviation 短縮　referendum 国民投票　ultimately 最終的に　come into play 作用する
be reluctant to V: ～するのを躊躇する　the British Commonwealth イギリス連邦　currency 通貨

2 ECSC 欧州石炭鉄鋼共同体　EEC 欧州経済共同体　EC 欧州共同体　EFTA 欧州自由貿易連合　apply for 申し込む　Charles de Gaulle シャルル・ド・ゴール　Pompidou ポンピドー　EU 欧州連合

3 <u>1. Sovereignty</u> 主権　cite 言及する　judicial 法律の　court system 裁判制度　uphold 守る
<u>2. Immigrants</u> considerable かなりの
<u>3. Economy</u> bear 負う　contribute 寄与する　budget 経費

4 contributor 寄与者　billion 十億　blow 打撃

【1】次の質問に日本語で答えよ。

1 1) 2016 年に行われた、Brexit についての国民投票の結果は？

2) EU 加盟後も UK が保持していた二つのものとは？

2 The “Inner Six” と the “Outer Seven” とは何か？

The “Inner Six” =

The “Outer Seven” =

3 1) Brexit の理由の一つである「主権」の問題とはどういうことか？

2) Brexit の理由の一つである「移民」の問題とはどういうことか？

3) Brexit の理由の一つである「経済」の問題とはどういうことか？

4 UK は EU でどのような位置にあったか？

【2】 Complete the following timetable in English

1951	ECSC (the European Coal and Steel Community)
1957	EEC (the European Economic Community)
1967	EC (European Community)
1973	UK joined the ([1]) with Denmark and ([2]).
1993	EU (European Union)
2016	A ([3]) conducted in the UK showed the support for Brexit.
2020	UK left EU (Brexit)

【3】 True or False

1) Brexit was officially carried out in 2020. (   )

2) The British people predominantly supported Brexit. (   )

3) The UK was at first reluctant to join the original body of EU because it still had strong relationships with the countries of its former Commonwealth. (   )

4) The UK accepted the "Euro," the EU currency, as its currency soon after it joined the EC. (   )

5) The order for the formation of the EU is, first, ECSC, then EEC, then EC, and finally EU. (   )

6) Switzerland is now an EU member. (   )

7) It was a big blow to the UK that many businesses left the UK due to Brexit. (   )

8) The British people wanted the EU to stop giving money to poor countries and to give more money to the U.K. (   )

9) The British people didn't want more immigrants because they were worried that the immigrants would take their jobs. (   )

10) Before Brexit, the UK had to pay a considerable amount of money to help poor countries in the EU. (   )

Episode 1 Scotland and Ireland over Brexit

Scotland

In 2014, Scotland held a referendum to decide if it wanted to become independent from the UK. The result was that 55% of Scottish voters voted to "Remain" in the UK. In a referendum for Brexit in 2016, 62% of Scottish voters voted to "Remain" in the EU, while England and Wales voted to "Leave." Northern Ireland also voted to "Remain." Now, many Scottish people are once again thinking about becoming independent from the UK.

Ireland

When the UK was in the EU, it refused to sign the Schengen Agreement, a treaty requesting the abolishment of national borders between member countries. Consequently, the UK kept the passport control when even EU members entered the UK. But the UK didn't apply this measure to the border between Ireland and Northern Ireland. Following the Good Friday Agreement (1998), which ended the Northern Ireland conflict, both countries agreed that the border would remain open. It's likely that the UK and Ireland will continue this policy, to avoid troubles.

1. Which countries voted to leave the EU?
   (1) England and Wales
   (2) England and Northern Ireland
   (3) Scotland and Northern Ireland
   (4) Scotland and Wales

2. How will Northern Ireland keep peace?
   (1) By leaving the border with Ireland unclear.
   (2) By joining the EU independently.
   (3) By joining Ireland.
   (4) By leaving the UK.

3. The Schengen Agreement requests the abolishment of …
   (1) taxes.
   (2) each country's parliament.
   (3) national borders.
   (4) each country's courts of law.

Notes

sign 署名する　the Schengen Agreement シェンゲン協定　abolishment 廃止　passport control 入国審査　apply 適用する　measure 措置　the Good Friday Agreement ベルファスト合意

Episode 2 Who supported Brexit?

According to a study conducted in 2017, the poorer areas of the UK tended to choose “Leave.” In those areas, there was a large influx of Eastern European immigrants, who, British people thought, took jobs away from native, low-skilled workers. People in the middle class voted for “Remain.” According to Thomas Sampson, “older and less-educated voters were more likely to vote to “Leave.” A majority of white voters wanted to “Leave.” There was no gender difference in the vote. Those who supported the Conservative Party tended to vote to “Leave,” thinking that life in Britain was getting worse due to the influx of immigrants. “Leave” voters hoped for a better immigration system, improved border controls, a fairer welfare system, a better quality of life, and the right to make and control their own laws. On the other hand, “Remain” voters hoped for a better economy, increased international investment, and greater UK influence on world affairs. Most of the pro-Brexit voters were older, working-class residents of England’s rural areas. Those who voted to stay in the EU lived primarily in London, Scotland, and Northern Ireland. Ethnic minorities generally voted to stay.

Which did the following groups tend to support “Leave” or “Remain”? For Leave, write “L.” For Remain, write “R.”

Example: areas that had lower incomes (L)

1. areas where there was a large influx of immigrants ( )
2. middle-class people ( )
3. older and less-educated people ( )
4. white voters ( )
5. Asians and Blacks ( )
6. supporters of the Conservative Party ( )

Notes

influx 流入　low-skilled worker 非熟練労働者　the Conservative Party 保守党　welfare system 福祉制度　investment 投資　resident 住民　primarily 主に

Unit

4

A Second Cold War?

US vs China

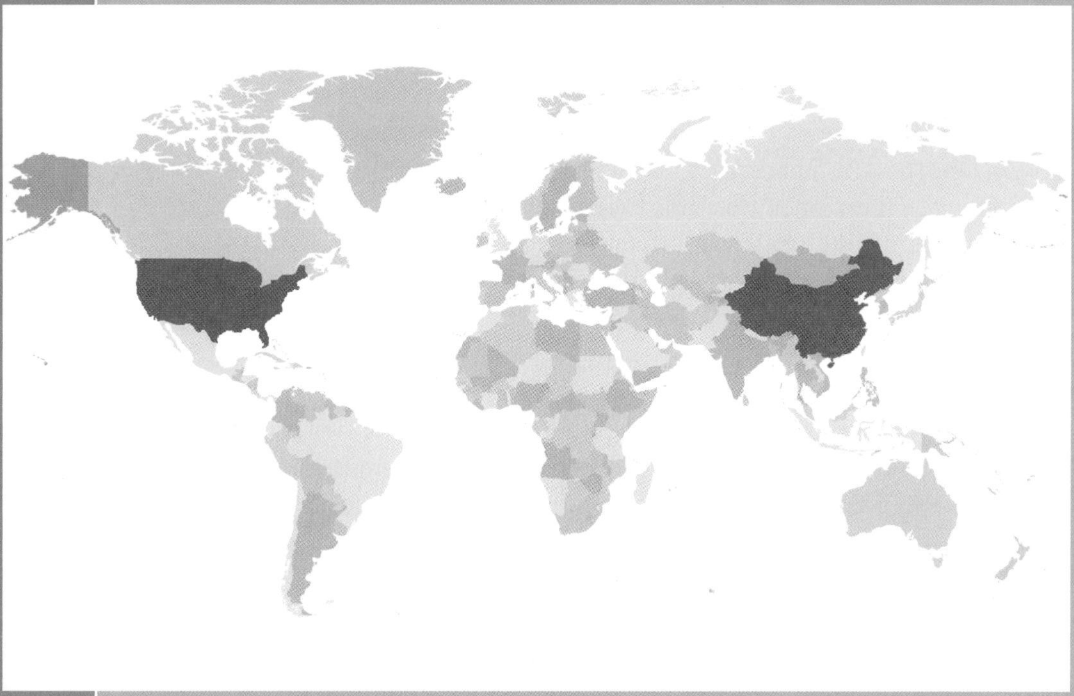

1. Which country was the US's rival during the Cold War era?
2. Which country is the US's new rival?
3. In which countries were wars fought during the Cold War era?
4. Who was the Russian president who helped end the Cold War?

1 **Outline** In 2019, the US announced that it was banning Huawei, a large Chinese communications company, from operating in America. This declaration sent shock waves around the world. Many people suspected that the US move would lead to a major confrontation between the two powers. The US was concerned that China would use Huawei's advanced technology to spy on the US. This concern was deepened when China stated its ambition of building a huge economic sphere covering Asia, Africa, and Europe. Fearing this economic expansion, the US has come to regard China as a major threat to American power and security. This situation has triggered an intense trade war between the two nations. It is unlikely that this friction will turn into an actual war, but a kind of economic and political "cold war" is definitely going on.

2 **The new Cold War?** The term Cold War, of course, refers to the decades-long political and economic tension between the US and the Soviet Union after the end of WWII. This war was thought to have ended with the dissolution of the Soviet Union in 1991. But now another cold war seems to be emerging, resulting from friction between the US and China. Some people are calling this growing tension the Second Cold War. Two points characterize this new Cold War. The most significant point is that the source of China's power is "economic rather than military." In the original Cold War (US vs the Soviet Union), the focus was on military competition, with the threat of nuclear weapons hanging in the background. Second, information technology is an important factor in this new cold war. Cyber-attacks will play a substantial role.

3 **History of relationship between the US and China** The US fought alongside China against Japan during the Pacific War. When WWII ended, China became a communist country, following the Soviet Union. In the subsequent Cold War, there was no real military conflict directly between the core countries, but there were some "hot" wars backed by two rival countries, for example, in Vietnam, Korea, Indochina, and so on. The US was in effect fighting indirectly against China through these wars. President Nixon visited China in 1972, and every US president, except for Carter, visited China. President Obama claimed China was of key importance. US-China relations worsened under President Trump, who regarded China as a threat. The US suspected that Chinese companies operating in the US might be spies working for the Chinese government. This led to a trade war and war of words and accusations. In 2020, the US accused China of spreading the coronavirus pandemic. Relations further deteriorated over China's oppression of Hong Kong and threats to Taiwan.

4 **Relationships between China and Russia** The relationship between China and Russia improved after the dissolution of the Soviet Union in 1991. The two countries share a long land border, which caused persistent territorial problems between them. They settled these border issues in 2001 when they signed the Treaty of Good Neighborliness and Friendly Cooperation. In the situation

where Russia has been pushed by the expansion of NATO and the EU, China is Russia's most important friend. In February 2022, Russia invaded Ukraine. Most countries criticized Russia's behavior, but China stood with Russia, saying that they understood Russia's actions. After all, the two countries are allies which are opposed to the same enemy: the US and the West.

5 **A new phase of the Cold War?** People thought that Russia would gradually fade away with the rise of China. But to most people's surprise, Russia invaded Ukraine in 2022. This extreme action was taken because Russia felt it was being pressured by the expansion of NATO, which implied victory for the western world and the US. The UN declared that it would not get involved in this issue, knowing its participation might lead to a Third World War and the use of nuclear weapons. The western world, however, supported Ukraine in various ways. Does this war signify the real end of the original Cold War, or is it a new phase of that Cold War, this time involving China?

Notes

1 ban 禁止する　confrontation 対立　be concerned 懸念する　spy スパイする　economic sphere 経済圏　trigger 誘発する　intense 激しい　friction 軋轢

2 tension 緊張　dissolution 解体　emerge 出現する　characterize 特徴付ける　hang 垂れ下がる　cyber-attack サイバー攻撃　substantial 重要な

3 subsequent それに続く（形）　worsen 悪化する　accusation 非難　accuse 非難する　coronavirus pandemic コロナ禍　deteriorate 悪化する　oppression 弾圧

4 persistent 持続する（形）　territorial 領土に関する　the Treaty of Good Neighborliness and Friendly Cooperation 中露善隣友好協力条約　ally 味方

5 phase 局面　signify 意味する

【1】次の質問に日本語で答えよ。

1 アメリカが中国の通信会社 Huawei を追放しようとした理由は？

2 第二次冷戦（中国対アメリカ）の特性を 2 つ指摘しなさい。

1.

2.

3 最近、アメリカと中国との関係を悪化させた事件とは何か？ 2 つ答えよ。

4 ロシアが現在中国を必要としている理由は？

5 国連が 2022 年のロシア・ウクライナ問題に関わらないと言った理由は？

【2】Choose the right answer.

1. China fought against ( ) in World War II.
   (1) the US (2) Japan (3) Korea (4) the UK

2. Which of these wars is not linked to the original Cold War?
   (1) Vietnam War (2) Korean War (3) Indochina War (4) World War II

3. Which president regarded China as a big threat?
   (1) Putin (2) Carter (3) Obama (4) Trump

【3】Complete the summary

After WWII, two superpowers emerged: the ([1]   ) and the Soviet Union. This was in many ways a war between capitalism and ([2]   ). There was no "hot war" between these two states, because of the threat of ([3]   ) weapons. With the ([4]   ) of the Soviet Union in 1991, the Cold War seemed to end. But now a new US rival has emerged; China. This might be called the "Second Cold War."

Episode 1 The Cold War

The Cold War (1947-1991) was political and economic tension between the Western Bloc (capitalist and democratic countries), led by the US, and the Eastern Bloc (communist and despotic countries), led by the Soviet Union. It began just after World War II ended, when the world saw that the two countries had emerged from the war as superpowers. It is generally said that this war began with the 1947 Truman Doctrine and ended with the 1991 dissolution of the Soviet Union.

This "cold war" got its name because there was no actual direct military fighting between the two superpowers, but they each took sides in regional conflicts, such as the Vietnam War, the Korean War, and the Indochina War. The Western Bloc formed NATO in 1949 and the Eastern Bloc established the Warsaw Pact in 1955 as military alliances.

In the 1980s, Soviet President Mikhail Gorbachev introduced the concepts of glasnost (openness) and perestroika (reorganization). Nationalism rose in the Eastern European countries, but Gorbachev did nothing to stop this movement. In 1989, the Berlin Wall between East and West Berlin was torn down by German people on both sides. The Baltic states declared their independence. Ukraine, the Caucasus, and the central Asian states also moved toward independence. In 1991, the Soviet Union finally collapsed and formally dissolved itself. People thought this was the end of the Cold War.

True or False

1) The original Cold War started during World War II. ( )
2) The Soviet Union and the US had become superpowers by the time World War II ended. ( )
3) In the original Cold War, the leader of the Western Bloc was the US and that of the Eastern Bloc was China. ( )
4) The Truman Doctrine is said to be the starting point of the Cold War. ( )
5) The time when the Soviet Union was dissolved is said to mark the end of the Cold War. ( )
6) There were some real military battles between the US and the Soviet Union during the Cold War. ( )

7) NATO and the Warsaw Pact were rival economic organizations. ( )

8) The Berlin Wall was torn down by the Soviet military. ( )

9) Michael Gorbachev suppressed the independence movements of the states that were under the control of the Soviet Union. ( )

10) It was Vladimir Putin who reformed the Soviet Union by introducing glasnost and perestroika. ( )

Notes

tension 緊張　bloc 圏　despotic 専制的な　superpower 超大国　Truman Doctrine トルーマン・ドクトリン　take sides どちらかの味方をする　the Warsaw Pact ワルシャワ条約機構　military alliance 軍事同盟　glasnost グラスノースチ　perestroika ペレストロイカ　tear down 倒す　collapse 倒れる　dissolve 解体する

Episode 2 The Belt and Road Initiative (BRI)

13

"The Belt and Road Initiative," known as "One Belt One Road," is a Chinese economic strategy adopted in 2013. It is an ambitious foreign policy announced by Xi Jinping, who originally called the strategy as the "Silk Road Economic Belt." By this name, he meant that all Asian countries should be connected economically as they had been over the old trade routes called "Silk Road." This plan includes the Middle East and Africa. China is planning to complete this project by 2049, which will coincide with the centennial anniversary of the foundation of the People's Republic of China. Some countries, with the US as leader, regard this initiative as a sinocentric international trade network. To improve their basic infrastructure, China has already invested billions of dollars in several South Asian countries like Pakistan, Nepal, Sri Lanka, Bangladesh, and Afghanistan. This could lead to China's establishment of a trade system along with military influence.

1. What is "One Belt One Road"?
   (1) A strategy to unite politically the area along the Silk Road.
   (2) A plan to build a long and well-equipped road to connect the West and the East
   (3) A plan to build an empire with China as its leader.
   (4) A plan to unite economically the area along the Silk Road.

2. Why is 2049 so important for China?
   (1) It marks the centennial anniversary of the rule by Xi Jinping.
   (2) It marks the centennial anniversary of the People's Republic of China
   (3) It marks the centennial anniversary of China's victory in World War II.
   (4) It marks the centennial anniversary of the opening of the new Silk Road.

3. How did the US and other Pacific countries react to the Belt and Road Initiative?
   (1) They welcomed this plan.
   (2) They regarded it as sinocentric.
   (3) They offered to build basic infrastructure for Asian countries.
   (4) They tried to pressure some Asian countries into rejecting this initiative.

Notes

The Belt and Road Initiative「一帯一路」 strategy 戦略　adopt 採用する　Xi Jinping 習近平　complete 完成させる　coincide with ～に一致する　centennial anniversary 百周年　initiative 構想　sinocentric 中国中心の　infrastructure インフラ・基本施設　invest 投資する　billion 10億

Unit
5

The Israeli-Palestinian Conflict

The most difficult global issue to resolve

1. Why do Israelis desperately want to have their own country?

2. Judaism, Christianity, Islam are called 'brother religions.' Why?

3. What is the capital city of Israel?

4. Who founded Palestine Liberation Organization (PLO)?

5. What is Hamas?

1 **Outline** The Israeli-Palestinian conflict is an old but current problem. It is probably the most difficult global issue to resolve. The conflict involves Palestinians, backed by Arab states, and Jewish people, backed by the US and other western nations, fighting to control the region called Palestine or Israel. The roots of this conflict trace back to the first century, when the Romans expelled Jewish people from Palestine, starting the Jewish diaspora. Palestinians have lived in this region since ancient times, possibly even before the Jews. The name 'Palestine' is from Philistines who lived there before the Jews arrived. Palestinians use this name to show their legitimacy to live there, although their connection with Philistines is not proved. In the 19th century, the rise of Zionism, a Jewish nationalist movement, prompted Jewish immigration to the region, and the Palestinians were pushed out. The British government promised a homeland to the Jewish people through the Balfour Declaration in 1917, expecting Jewish people would fight against the Ottoman Empire. More Jews entered Palestine. The conflict heated up after WWII because of the experience of the Holocaust. In 1948, Jewish people declared the establishment of the 'State of Israel', and in 1988, Palestinians declared the 'State of Palestine,' and the two are still in conflict today.

2 **Ethnicity, language and religion** Jews are an ethnoreligious group who originate from the ancient Hebrews, and whose religion is Judaism. Jews worship Yahweh, the one and only God. Their main language is Hebrew, a Northwest Semitic language. Modern Palestinians mostly come from the ancient Levantines, and they followed Judaism, Christianity, and later Islam. Although they claim a connection to the ancient Philistines, who lived around the area that is now Gaza, the present Palestinians are Arabs. Over the centuries, they were conquered by many empires, and in the 7th century, with the arrival of Muslims, they underwent Arabization and Islamization. As a result, modern day Palestinian ethnicity is a mixture of various peoples.

3 **History** In the 10th century BC, the Israelite kingdoms of Israel and Judah ruled much of Palestine, while the Philistines occupied its southern coast. Since then, Palestine has been controlled by many kingdoms and empires, including the Persian Empire, Alexander the Great, the Roman Empire, several Muslim empires, and Crusaders. The Ottoman Empire governed the area from 1517. Jews were expelled from this region by the Romans around the first century. Those who stayed in this region accepted Christianity under Roman rule and then Islam under Arab empires, becoming modern-day Palestinians. The Jews who left the region tried to settle in other countries but faced persecution. In the 19th century, they started to return to their 'Promised Land', which is the land where Palestinians have long lived. After the Ottoman Empire collapsed at the end of WWI, the League of Nations gave Britain mandatory power over Palestine in 1922. There were many conflicts between Arabs and Jews. After WWII, this escalated because Jews desperately desired their own country due to their

experience of the Holocaust. In 1947, Britain ended the mandate, leading to the declaration of the State of Israel in 1948. Approximately 700,000 Palestinians, about 80% of the population, fled or were driven out (Palestinian diaspora). Starting in the late 1940s, about 850,000 Jews immigrated to Israel. In the end, only two parts of Palestine remained in Arab control: the West Bank and the Gaza Strip. These regions were conquered by Israel during the Six-Day War in 1967. Despite international objections, Israel started to establish settlements in these occupied territories.

4 **Zionism and Palestinian Nationalism** Zionism is a nationalist movement among Jewish people. Palestinian nationalism, on the other hand, emerged in response to Zionism during the 19th century. The term 'Palestine' started to be used in this period. In 1964, Yasser Arafat established the Palestinian Liberation Organization (PLO), which is recognized globally as the official representative of the Palestinian people. Initially, the PLO did not recognise Israel. However, in 1993, it recognized Israel as part of the Oslo Accord. Following Arafat's death in 2004, Fatah, the ruling party, lost the 2006 election to Hamas. Hamas, considered a terrorist organization by many countries, does not recognize Israel and gained control of Gaza in 2007. The PLO rules only the West Bank. In October 2023, Hamas launched a surprise attack on southern Israel, and Israeli responded with a brutal assault of the Gaza Strip.

5 **The Israeli-Palestinian issue and the United Nations** The UN proposed a partition plan for Palestine, suggesting the establishment of 'an independent Arab State, an independent Jewish State, and the City of Jerusalem'. In 1948, Israel declared its statehood, which led Arab states to invade the region (The First Arab-Israeli War). As a result, Israel gained further territory and in 1949 was admitted into the UN on the condition that it accepts the Partition Plan. In 1988, Palestine declared its independence, becoming the State of Palestine. While the UN has not officially recognized this state, the UN has granted it 'non-member observer State' status. The UN has criticized Israel's settlement activities as illegal, but the US has consistently defended Israel.

Notes

1 trace back to ～に遡る　expel 追放する　diaspora 離散　Philistines フィリシテ人　legitimacy 正当性　Zionism シオニズム　prompt 推進する　Holocaust ホロコースト（ナチスによるユダヤ人大虐殺）

2 ethnoreligious 民族宗教的　originate from ～に起源を持つ　Hebrew ヘブライ人　Judaism ユダヤ教　Yahweh ヤハウェ　Levantine レバント人

3 Crusaders 十字軍　persecution 迫害　mandatory 委任統治

4 initially 最初は　the Oslo Accord オスロ合意　launch 始める　assault 襲撃

5 partition 分割　statehood 国家　The First Arab-Israeli War「第一次中東戦争」　illegal 不法の　consistently ずっと　defend 擁護する

【1】次の質問に日本語で答えよ。

1 ユダヤ人の離散はいつ始まったか？

2 現在のパレスチナ人の民族性を説明せよ。

3 1) 第二次世界大戦でオスマン帝国が崩壊し、パレスチナの地は誰が統治したか？

2) パレスチナ人の離散は何がきっかけか？

4 1) パレスチナ人のアイデンティは何がきっかけか？

2) PLO とハマスの決定的な違いは何か？

5 1) 国連のパレスチナ分割案とは？

2) 国連でのパレスチナとイスラエルの位置は？

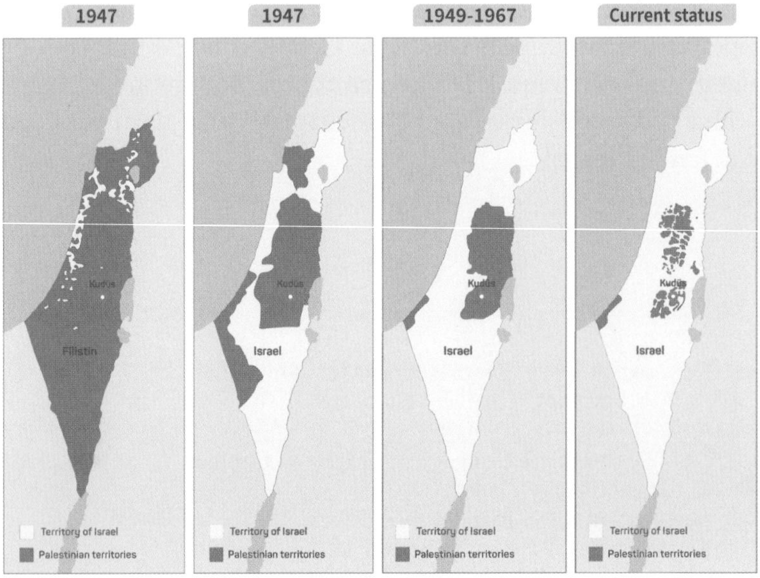

https://ccp-ngo.jp/palestine/palestine-information/

【2】Complete the following timetable in English

BC.12C	Philistines came to Palestine (then Canaan)
BC.10C	Israelite kingdoms were built: ([1]) and Judah
AD.1-2C	([2]) expelled the Jews → Jewish diaspora
7C	Palestine region was Islamized
1517-WWI	Under the rule of the Ottoman Empire
1917	([3]) Declaration: Britain promised a homeland to Jewish people.
1922-1948	British Mandate over former Ottoman territory
1947	UN proposed the Partition Plan
1948	Jewish people declared the State of ([4])
1964	PLO was founded.
1988	Palestinians declared the State of Palestine
1993	The Oslo accords: PLO recognized Israel
2006-2007	Hamas won the election and took over Gaza
2004	([5]) attacked Israel from Gaza

【3】True or False

1) Palestinians are supported by Arab states and the US. ( )
2) Jewish diaspora started when they were expelled by Israelis in the first century. ( )
3) The name 'Palestinians' is from 'Philisitis' (Philistines). ( )
4) Zionism started in the 20th century. ( )
5) Christianity, Judaism and Islam worship the same God. ( )
6) Palestinias have been Arabs from the beginning. ( )
7) Palestinian identity was formed in response to Zionism. ( )
8) PLO and Hamas don't recognize Israel as the state. ( )
9) PLO now rules only the Gaza Strip. ( )
10) Palestine declared the establishment of the State of Palestine in 1988, but it is not yet recognized by the UN. ( )

Episode 1 Britain's three-tongued diplomacy

In WWI, the Ottoman Empire allied with Germany and was at war with Britain. To win the war and gain the territories under the Ottoman Empire, especially Palestine, Britain used the notorious 'three-tongued diplomacy.' To gain support, Britain offered contradictory proposals to three groups: Arabs, Jews, and France. None of these were part of parliamentary debates; they were conducted secretly.

1) McMahon-Hussein Correspondence (1915-16)

These are the letters exchanged between Sir Henry McMahon, the British High Commissioner in Cairo, and the ruler of Hejaz, Emir Hussein. The UK Government agreed to recognize Arab independence in a large region after the war in exchange for the Arab revolt against the Ottoman Empire.

2) Sykes-Picot Agreement (1916)

This was a secret wartime agreement between Britain and France, negotiated by Mark Sykes, the Conservative MP, and Francois Georges-Picot, the French High Commissioner. The aim of Sykes-Picot was the division of the Middle East between Britain and France (later Russia joined).

3) Balfour Declaration (1917)

This declaration announced its support for the establishment of a 'national home for the Jewish people' in Palestine. The declaration was contained in a letter from UK's Foreign Secretary Arthur Balfour to Lord Rothschild, a leader of the British Jewish community. This declaration was published in 1917.

These three agreements contradict each other. Giving an independent state to the Arabs (Palestinians), sharing the former Ottoman territories with France, and allowing Jewish people to establish their 'national home' in Palestine were impossible to carry out at the same time. These contradictory agreements made by Britain have contributed to the Palestinian conflicts and are now severely criticized.

1. By McMahon-Hussein Correspondence, Britain expected …
   (1) Arabs would become independent after WWI.
   (2) Arabs would rebel against the Ottoman Empire.
   (3) Arabs would be ruled by Britain.
   (4) Arabs would be united.

2. The Balfour Declaration promised that …
   (1) Britain would expel Palestinians from Palestine.
   (2) Jewish people could live in Palestine under British rule.
   (3) Palestinians would have their independent state.
   (4) Jewish people could establish their homeland in Palestine.

3. Britain's 'three-tongued' diplomacy …
   (1) led to the decline of the British Empire.
   (2) led to the current Israeli-Palestinian conflict.
   (3) has been praised by other countries.
   (4) solved many problems.

Notes

Three-tongued diplomacy 三枚舌外交　**ally** 同盟する　**notorious** 悪名高い　**contradictory** 矛盾した　**parliamentary** 議会の　**High Commissioner** 高等弁務官　**Hejaz** ヒジャズ（アラビア半島の王国）　**in exchange for** ～と交換に　**revolt** 反乱　**contain** 含む　**Foreign Secretary** 外相　**Lord Rothschild** ロスチャイルド卿　**contradict** 矛盾する　**contribute** 寄与する・引き起こす

Episode 2 Jerusalem

Jerusalem has been regarded as a holy city by three monotheistic religions, namely Judaism, Christianity, and Islam. In principle, these three religions are brothers. These are called the Abrahamic religions, centred around the worship of the same God. According to Judaism, there are many messengers of God. In Judaism, Abraham and Moses are messengers. In Christianity, Jesus is recognized as the best messenger (messiah). In Islam, Muhammad is recognized as the last messenger (prophet). All three religions consider Jerusalem a holy city, leading to numerous conflicts. For Jewish people, this city was built by King David as the capital of Israel. This place has been the central symbol for the Jewish people. For Christians, Jerusalem is significant as the place where Jesus was crucified and resurrected. In Islam, it is believed that Muhammad ascended to heaven from Jerusalem, making the city holy along with Mecca and Medina. This city is only 0.9 km^2, but it is a very important place. Today, the status of Jerusalem remains one of the core issues in the Israeli-Palestinian conflict. During the 1948 Arab-Israeli War, West Jerusalem was annexed by Israel, while East Jerusalem was annexed by Jordan. During the 1967 Six-Day War, Israel annexed the East. However, the UN rejects this as illegal and regards East Jerusalem as Palestinian territory occupied by Israel. While Tel Aviv is currently Israel's capital, Israel has long wanted to transfer its capital to Jerusalem. In 2017, US President Donald Trump announced that the US would recognize Jerusalem as the capital of Israel and, in 2018, transferred the US embassy from Tel Aviv to Jerusalem. The US's consistent support for Israel has invited criticism from the international community.

1. Which statement is true?
   (1) Jesus was born in Jerusalem.
   (2) Muhammad is God.
   (3) Abraham is a prophet.

2. Jerusalem is now …
   (1) Israel's capital city.
   (2) Palestine's capital city.
   (3) divided into two.

Notes

Monotheistic 一神教の　**namely** つまり　**in principle** 原理上
messengers 使者　**Moses** モーゼ　**numerous** 多くの　**crucify** 磔刑にする
ascend 昇る　**annex** 併合する　**currently** 現在では　**transfer** 移す　**consistent** 変わらない・徹底した

Unit 6

Rohingya

A troubled minority in Myanmar

Hundreds of thousands of Rohingya have left their ethnic homeland of Rakhine State for the district of Cox's Bazar in Chittagong, Bangladesh.

Cox's Bazar in Chittagong, Bangladesh

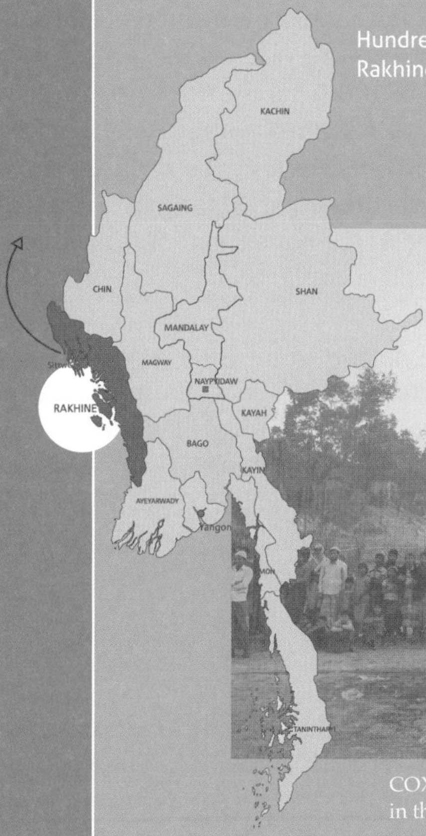

COX'S BAZAR, JANUARY 26 2018 — Muslim Rohingya waiting the foods in the refugee camp at balukhali Bangladesh.

1. In which country do the Rohingya people mainly live?
2. What was the old name of Myanmar?
3. Who is the world-wide famous female politician and the Nobel Peace Prize winner from Myanmar?
4. What's Rohingya people's religion?

1 **Outline** In 2015, to escape persecution and violence, thousands of Rohingya people fled Myanmar and Bangladesh. But most of the countries in which they sought refuge refused to accept them. The terrible scenes of crowded boats filled with Rohingya refugees drifting on the open sea were seen by millions of people on TV around the world. The Rohingya are an Indo-Aryan ethnic group who follow the religion of Islam. They live in the state of Rakhine, in the western part of Myanmar. The UN has called the Rohingya one of the most persecuted minority peoples in the world. Under the 1982 Myanmar Citizenship law, the Rohingya are not regarded as true Myanmar citizens. The government of Myanmar restricts their freedom of movement, denies their children a state education, and prohibits them from holding civil-service jobs.

2 **Ethnicity and religion** The Rohingya people belong to an Indo-Aryan ethnic group. They practice a mixture of Sunni Islam and Sufism. They claim that they are a people indigenous to an area of western Myanmar called "Arakan." The Myanmar government insists that the Rohingya are not Arakan's indigenous people, but that they are illegal immigrants from Bangladesh. The Myanmar government calls them "Bengali." This conflict and tension have led the Rohingya to several armed riots against the government since the 1940s.

3 **History** It is not precisely clear who the indigenous people of Arakan were. Arakan is the ancient name of a region along the Bay of Bengal, which is now called Rakhine. The region has been a key center of trade and cultural exchange between Burma (the old colonial name of Myanmar) and the world. The earliest Muslim settlements in Arakan began in the 7th century. By the 8th century, Arab traders had converted the local Buddhist people to Islam. This conversion was accelerated by marriages between the Arab traders and the local people. In the 18th century, the British came and occupied this area. Many Muslim people living in Arakan fled to other countries. In the early 19th century, thousands of Bengalis from southeastern Bengal settled in Arakan, seeking work. Whether those new migrants from Bengal were the same people who had fled to Bengal when the British conquered Arakan in the 18th century is not known. But if they were the same people, the Rohingya's claim that they were the indigenous people of Arakan might be reasonable. Burma became a province within the British Indian Empire. Burma came under Japanese rule in 1942, but it was formally recognized as an independent country in 1948.

4 **British diplomacy connected to Rohingya problem after WWII** The attitude and policy of the British toward Muslims and Buddhists in Burma in the days after WWII are not clear. Muslim leaders claimed that the British rulers had promised to establish a "Muslim National Area" for them in the Arakan region. When the war ended, a considerable number of illegal Muslim immigrants entered this area, believing the British had promised a land for them.

5 **The 1978 incident** In 1962, a military junta seized control of Burma. Under the new military government, the Rohingya people were repeatedly deprived of their political rights. Then, starting in 1978, the junta systematically attacked the Rohingya people. Over 200,000 Rohingya people fled to Bangladesh, but the Bangladesh government refused them. One report says that 12,000 people died. Bangladesh signed an agreement with Burma stating that most refugees should be returned to Burma under the control of UNHCR, the United Nations refugees agency.

6 **Recent developments** In 1982, the junta enacted a new citizenship law in which the Rohingya were not listed as one of the 135 "national races" of Burma. This meant that the Rohingya people in Burma became essentially stateless. In 1989, Burma officially renamed itself "Myanmar," and in the 1990s, Arakan was renamed as Rakhine State. Since the passage of the 1982 citizenship law, Burmese juntas and governments have strongly objected to the use of the term "Rohingya," calling the people "illegal immigrants." In the 1990s, a new Rohingya movement emerged, which used overseas refugees to spread the Rohingya's indigenous claims and made sure the term "Rohingya" should be known to the world. In 2012, some 140,000 Rohingya people in Myanmar were confined in camps. In 2015, thousands of Rohingya people fled Myanmar and Bangladesh, many of them becoming "boat people." In 2017, Myanmar security forces began what they called "clearance operations" against the Rohingya in northern Rakhine State. The UN Security Council issued a statement calling the action an example of "ethnic cleansing."

Notes

1 persecution 迫害　flee-fled-fled 逃れる　drift 漂流する　persecute 迫害する　deny 否定する　Myanmar Citizenship law ミャンマー国籍法　restrict 制限する　civil service job 公務員

2 Sunni Islam スンニ派イスラム　Sufism スーフィズム（イスラム神秘主義）　indigenous 土着の　illegal 不法の　armed riot 武装暴動

3 precisely 正確に　convert 改宗させる　conversion 改宗　accelerate 加速させる　migrant 移民

5 military junta 軍事政権　seize 握る　deprive A of B　A から B を奪う　systematically 組織的に　UNHCR 国連難民高等弁務官事務所

6 enact 制定する　list リストに載せる　confine 閉じ込める　camp 収容所　security forces 治安部隊　clearance operations 民族浄化作戦　the UN Security Council 国連安全保障理事会　issue 出す　statement 声明　ethnic clearance 民族浄化

【1】次の質問に日本語で答えよ。

1 1982年のMyanmar nationality lawではRohingyaをどう位置付けているか?

2 Rohingyaの出自について、Rohingya側とMyanmar側の主張はどう違うか?

3 19世紀に多くのベンガル人がArakanに定住したが、これがRohingyaの問題とどういう関係があるか?

4 第二次大戦後多くのムスリム移民がアラカンに入ってきたが、なぜか?

5 1978年事件の原因とその結果を答えなさい。

6 1990年代の新しい動きとはどういうものか?

【2】Complete the following timetable in English

7C	The earliest Muslim people entered and settled in Arakan.
8C	Arab traders converted the local Buddhist people to ([1]).
18C 19C	The ([2]) occupied Arakan. → Many Muslim people left Arakan. → Bengali people migrated into Arakan.
1962	Burma's military junta
1978	The Burmese junta government attacked Rohingya people.
1982	The ([3]) law was enacted → Rohingya were excluded from the 135 'national races' of Burma.
2015	Many Rohingya fled Myanmar and Bangladesh. → "Boat people"
2017	Myanmar security forces began "([4]) operations" against the Rohingya.

【3】True or False

1) The Rohingya people are an Indo-Aryan ethnic group and follow Islam. ( )

2) The Myanmar government at first denied that the Rohingya were the indigenous people of Arakan, but they now accept the Rohingya as the region's indigenous people. ( )

3) During 2017-2018, many Rohingya people fled to Bangkok. ( )

4) The UN criticized Myanmar for killing many Rohingya people, calling it "ethnic cleansing." ( )

5) Britain used the Rohingya to drive Bengali people away from Arakan. ( )

6) In 2015, thousands of Rohingya people fled Myanmar to Bangladesh. ( )

7) Most Rohingya people are now Buddhists. ( )

8) Many Rohingya people were Buddhists before they converted to Islam. ( )

9) In 1978, persecuted Rohingya people fled to Bangladesh and were soon accepted there as refugees. ( )

10) In 1982, the Myanmar government excluded the Rohingya from the "national citizenship" list, calling them "illegal immigrants." ( )

Episode 1 Aung San Suu Kyi

Aung San Suu Kyi is a Nobel Peace Prize winner (1991). She spent the period between 1989 and 2010 in detention because of her activities to restore democracy to military-ruled Myanmar. She was released in 2010, and led the National League for Democracy (NLD), which won the election in 2015. She was not allowed to become president, because according to the country's election laws, any person who is married to a foreigner could not become president. She was at the time married to a British scholar. Suu Kyi became a "state counsellor" in 2016. Her attitude toward the Rohingya issue was controversial. She faced criticism for not speaking out for the Rohingya, which put her in an awkward position. If she had officially supported the Rohingya, it would have caused a reaction from Buddhist nationalists and military officials. Her lack of support for the Rohingya gave rise to considerable criticism from people in the world. Some organizations cancelled the prizes she had been awarded. In February 2021, there was a coup d'etat and the military junta came back to power and Aung San Suu Kyi was arrested by the military and was put under house arrest again.

1. Aung San Suu Kyi was in detention for around …
   (1) twenty years.
   (2) ten years.
   (3) fifteen years.
   (4) one and half years.

2. Aung San Suu Kyi was not qualified to become president because …
   (1) she was a woman.
   (2) she had been arrested.
   (3) she had a British husband.
   (4) she was against the government.

3. Aung San Suu Kyi was criticized by foreign countries, because …
   (1) she didn't stand in the presidential election.
   (2) she actively suppressed the Rohingya people.
   (3) she didn't do anything to help the Rohingya people.
   (4) she stopped participating in politics.

Notes

detention 拘留　restore 復活させる　release 解放する　the National League for Democracy 国民民主連盟　state counsellor 国家顧問　controversial 物議を醸すような　criticism 批判　awkward 気まずい　coup d'etat クーデター　put ~ under house arrest ～を自宅軟禁状態に置く

Episode 2 Japan and the Rohingya

During WWII, the Japanese Army invaded the then British-controlled country of Burma and British forces had to retreat from Arakan. The British supported the Muslims, so there was considerable violence between Arakanese Buddhists and Muslims after the departure of the British. When the Japanese, who supported the Buddhists, invaded Burma, the Muslims were forced to flee towards British-controlled, Muslim-dominated northern Arakan. A large number of Buddhists living in northern Arakan were consequently attacked and killed by Muslims. The British provided the Rohingya people with arms hoping that they would fight against the Japanese army, but the Rohingya people used those arms to attack Buddhists.

1. During WWII in Arakan, …
   (1) the Japanese supported the Buddhists.
   (2) the British supported the Buddhists.
   (3) the Japanese at first supported the Buddhists, but at the end of the war, they supported Muslims.
   (4) the British supported both the Buddhists and the Muslims.

2. Which statement is true?
   (1) The Japanese army gave arms to the Rohingya, but they used them to fight against Japanese forces.
   (2) The Japanese army's plan was to make the Rohingya fight against the British, but the Rohingya attacked the Buddhists in Arakan.
   (3) Rohingya people were given arms by the British to fight against the Japanese army, but they used them to fight against Buddhists in Arakan.
   (4) The British people provided the Rohingya people with arms, expecting them to drive the Buddhists away.

Notes

retreat 退却する　arms 武器

Unit

7 Basques

The oldest European people

1. In which European country do the majority of Basques live?

2. The capital city of Catalonia is Barcelona. How much do you know about Barcelona?

3. Which famous city was bombed in WWII and became the subject of a famous painting by Picasso?

1 **Outline** Spain today is made up of 17 autonomous regions. In the year 711, the Iberian Peninsula was invaded by Muslims. This occupation lasted until January 1492. That's when the Reconquista—the long war against their Islamic rulers—was completed with the fall of the city of Granada. Most of Spain's 17 autonomous communities came into being with the end of the Reconquista. One of these regions was Basque Country. The Basques have a unique and distinct language and ethnicity, which has resulted in various conflicts over the centuries. They have been persecuted and their language and culture suppressed, which has given rise to a modern separatist movement.

2 **Ethnicity, language and religion** Basques are the oldest surviving ethnic group in Europe. They are a Southwestern European ethnic group, although scholars have not yet determined the exact origins of the Basques. Their language is isolated, and there is no evidence of any connection with other languages. "Basque" is the last remaining descendant of the pre-Indo-European languages of prehistoric Europe. The indigenous Basque language is still spoken by 28.4% (751,500) of Basques in all the territories in which they are found. Of these, 93.2% are in the Spanish area of Basque Country, and the remaining 6.8% are in the French portion. Most Basques today are Roman Catholic.

3 **History** Much of Basque history is still largely a mystery. The Vascones, a group of people who lived in Northern Spain, are thought to be related to the Basques, whose name was probably given to them by the Vascones. When the Romans invaded the Iberian Peninsula in the first century BC, the Basques had probably lived in the Pyrenees for thousands of years. This area, because it was mountainous and not at all fertile, was not so attractive to the Romans. Owing to these geographical features, the Basques were never attacked by the Visigoths, Muslims, or Franks. By the 10th century, the territories where the Basques lived had been incorporated into the Kingdom of Navarre. The Iberian Peninsula was united during the Reconquista under Castile and Aragon. The Basque territory was conquered by Castilian forces in the 1500s. The Basques were given autonomy, but then in the 19th century, Spain and France both began to pressure the Basques into assimilating. It was during this period that Basque nationalism became increasingly intense.

4 **WWII** In the 1930s, during the Spanish Civil War, Basque culture was suppressed by Spain's leader Franco and his fascist party. Franco tried to get rid of all heterogeneity in Spain, and the Basque people were especially targeted. The Basques were systematically deprived of their political autonomy and economic rights. Many Basques were imprisoned or killed. In 1937, Guernica, a Basque town, was severely bombed and badly damaged with several hundred civilians killed. When Franco died in 1975, the Basques once again regained their autonomy.

5 **Terrorism** In 1959, ETA, a Basque nationalist or terrorist group, was founded. Their aim was to secure Basque independence. Since then this separatist and socialist organization conducted terrorist activities to break away from Spain and France. Over 800 people were killed through assassinations and terrorist bombings. Weary of such brutality, today most Basque people do not support the violent activities of ETA. Furthermore, not all Basques want complete sovereignty or independence.

6 **Basques under France and Spain** Both the Spanish and French governments have, at times, suppressed Basque language, culture, and identity. France demanded the assimilation of all minority groups, emphasizing its one-nation policy. Spain, in contrast, has granted some degree of autonomy to the Basques. Today, the Basque Country within Spain enjoys extensive political and cultural autonomy. But in the Basque Country in France, Basques are not officially recognized. Their autonomy is suppressed and they are subjected to monolingual (French) public schooling.

Notes

1 autonomous region 自治区　the Iberian Peninsula イベリア半島　the Reconquista レコンキスタ（国土回復運動）　complete 完成する　distinct 独特の　suppress 抑圧する　give rise to ～を引き起こす　separatist movement 分離運動

2 scholar 学者　determine 決定する・判断する　descendant 子孫　prehistoric 先史時代の

3 mountainous 山岳の　fertile 肥沃な　Visigoths 西ゴート人　Navarre ナバレ　autonomy 自治　assimilate 同化する　intense 激しい

4 the Spanish Civil War スペイン内戦　heterogeneity 異端性・異質性　imprison 投獄する

5 found 設立する　separatist 分離主義の　assassination 暗殺　be weary of ～にうんざりする

6 assimilation 同化　extensive 広範囲の　monolingual 単一言語での　public schooling 公的教育

【1】次の質問に日本語で答えよ。

1 バスクはスペインの 17 の自治州の一つであるが、これらの自治州はいつ出来上がったか？

2 バスク人の言語の特徴を指摘しなさい。

3 バスク地方がローマ人に侵略されなかったのはなぜか？

4 1930 年代、フランコはなぜバスク人を排除しようとしたのか？

5 ETA とは何か？

6 フランスのバスク人の扱い方とスペインのバスク人の扱い方との違いを答えよ。

【2】Complete the following timetable in English

1C.BC	the ([1]) invaded the Iberian Peninsula.
Middle Ages	The Basques were incorporated into Navare.
1500s	Castilian forces conquered the Basque territory.
19C	Basque ([2]) became intense.
WWII	The Basque people were persecuted by the ([3]) government.
1975	The Basques received their ([4]).
1959	Some of the fiercest Basque nationalists founded ETA.

【3】True or False

1) The Iberian Peninsula was conquered by Muslims and this period was called the Reconquista. ( )
2) Basque Country is excluded from Spain's 17 autonomous regions. ( )
3) It is believed that the Basque people are the oldest surviving ethnic group in Europe. ( )
4) The Basque language is unique in that it is not connected to any other language. ( )
5) More Basque speakers live in Spain than in France. ( )
6) The Romans wanted the Basque area because it is flat and fertile. ( )
7) Franco hated the fact that Spain had various ethnic elements and thus tried to get rid of the Basques. ( )
8) Guernica was bombed by Nazi Germany. ( )
9) ETA is a Basque nationalist organization whose aim is to free the Basques from Spain and France. ( )
10) The Basques who live in Spain enjoy more freedom than those who live in France. ( )

Episode 1 The Basque Country and Catalonia

Catalonia is an autonomous region located in northeast Spain. The Catalans belong to a Romance ethnic group native to Catalonia. The Basque Country and Catalonia are Spain's most extreme and fanatically nationalist regions. Generally, however, the independence movement of the Basques is less fierce than that of Catalonia. Why?

Traditionally, it was the Basques who desired autonomy and independence most earnestly. But now, the Basques' aim is to gain full autonomy inside Spain rather than full independence, while the Catalans are apt to seek independence.

Several factors can be pointed out to explain this difference. The first factor is the history of fanatical terrorist activity in the Basque Country, which has made the people tired of violence, and want peace. Second, the Basques are granted a system of fiscal autonomy called the Basque Economic Agreement. This system has not been given to Catalonia, partly because Catalonia is a territory rich in resources, and the Spanish government needs the financial rewards from Catalonia.

Spain is a country made up of many autonomous regions, with each region claiming its autonomy and identity. This situation resulted from the fact that it was very difficult to unify the many separate regions of the Iberian Peninsula. The Basque Country and Catalonia are the most visible examples of this difficulty.

1. What do the Basque Country and Catalonia have in common?
   (1) language
   (2) ethnicity
   (3) nationalism
   (4) history

2. Which statement is NOT true?
   (1) Historically, the desire for independence on the Basque side was stronger than that of Catalonia.
   (2) The Basques are now more fanatical than the Catalonians in their desire for independence.
   (3) Currently, the desire for independence is stronger in Catalonia than in the Basque Country.
   (4) The Basques' current aim is to gain full autonomy rather than full independence.

3. Which is NOT a reason for the difference between the Basque Country and Catalonia?
   (1) a different fiscal system
   (2) a different history and experience of terrorism
   (3) different ethnic characteristics

Notes

a Romance ethnic group ロマンス民族グループ　native to 〜に土着の　fanatically 狂信的に　fierce 激しい　be apt to V Vする傾向にある　grant 与える　fiscal 税制の　reward 報酬　visible 目に見える

Episode 2 **Guernica**

Guernica is a town in the Basque Country of Spain. On April 26, 1937, Guernica was bombed by Nazi Germany. Irritated by the resistance of Guernica, Franco, the leader of the Spanish nationalists asked Nazi Germany to attack this city. The attack was aimed at destroying the Basque government and Franco's enemies: the Spanish Republican elements. During the Spanish Civil War (1936-1939), the Republicans fought against Franco's nationalists. The Republican forces were, in fact, made up of various factions, including communists, socialists, anarchists, and others, all with different goals. They were united under one goal: to defeat the fascists led by General Franco, who sought a return to a pre-Republican Spain based on law, order, and traditional Catholic values. Guernica was seen as the northern base of the Republican resistance movement as well as the center of Basque culture. Spanish fascists aimed to protect traditional Spanish value systems and to exclude all others, which is why Guernica became the target of the Spanish fascists. The bombing of Guernica is considered to be the origin of the concept of terrorist bombings, where civilian targets were purposely selected as a way to discourage the enemy. The great Spanish artist Pablo Picasso painted "Guernica," one of the most famous paintings of the 20th century, to commemorate the horrors of the bombing.

1. Nazi Germany bombed Guernica because …
   (1) Franco, a fascist Spanish leader of Spain, asked Nazi Germany to bomb the town.
   (2) the Nazis made a mistake.
   (3) the Nazis was planning to invade and conquer Spain.
   (4) the Nazis thought the Basques would be a threat to them.

2. Many civilians were targeted for bombing in Guernica, because …
   (1) many Basque civilians were fighting against Franco.
   (2) Franco planned to wipe out the Basque people.
   (3) Guernica's soldiers were not real Basques.
   (4) Nazi Germany wanted to make the Basque people give up fighting.

3. Pablo Picasso made his work "Guernica" because …
   (1) Guernica was his hometown.
   (2) he hoped people around the world would remember how terrible this incident was.
   (3) he was in Guernica when Guernica was bombed.
   (4) he wanted to raise money to help the people of Guernica recover from the bombing.

Notes

faction 党派　anarchist 無政府主義者　value system 価値体系　exclude 排除する　civilian 民間人の
commemorate 後世に伝える・追悼する

Unit
8

Korea

The division of Korea

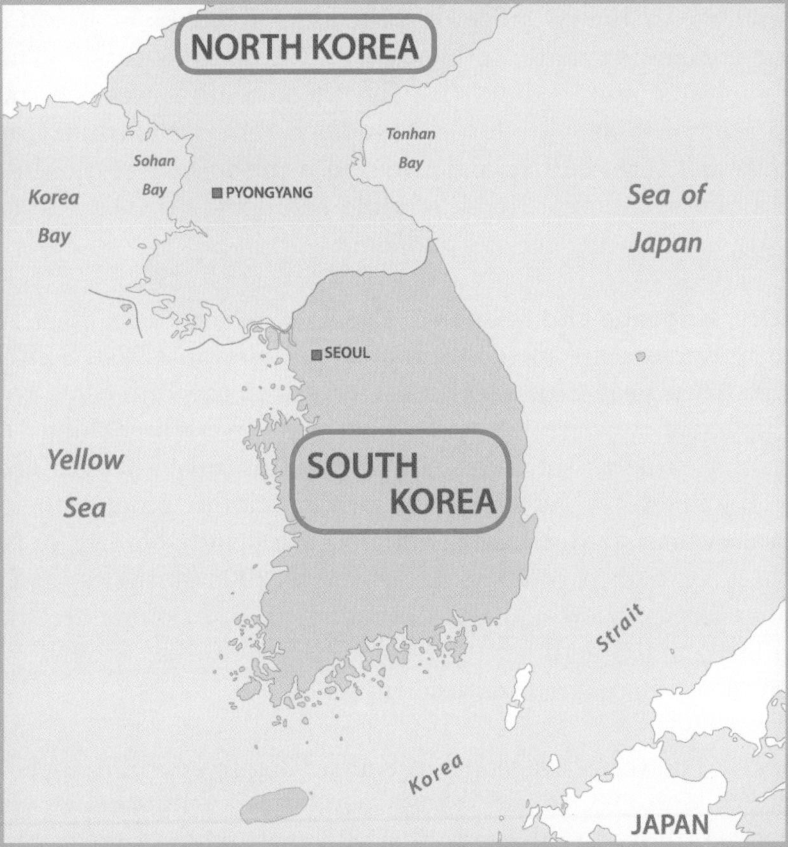

1. Why is the Korean peninsula divided into two separate countries?

2. Who is the current leader of North Korea?

3. What is the line called that divides North Korea and South Korea?

1 **Outline** Korea is a peninsula in East Asia that faces the Yellow Sea and Sea of Japan. Since 1945, the peninsula has been split across the middle into two countries: North Korea, officially known as the Democratic People's Republic of Korea; and South Korea, officially called the Republic of Korea. The former is a despotic communist state, influenced by China and Russia. The latter is a democratic capitalist state siding with the US and other western countries. The two Koreas' relationships with Japan have been very complicated. Japan invaded Korea twice in the 16th century and annexed it in the early 20th century. Japan's annexation and occupation of Korea and the peninsula's division after the Second World War are now causing serious problems.

2 **Ethnicity, language and religion** Koreans belong to an East Asian ethnic group. Modern Koreans are the descendants of immigrants from Southern Siberia. Originally, Koreans used Chinese characters, but in the 15th century, the Hangul script was invented to write Korean, which made recording things much easier. As for religion, Confucianism, Taoism, and Buddhism dominated Korea for a long time, but in the middle of the 20th century, Christianity entered the country, and now it is as prevalent as Buddhism. Religion is officially banned in North Korea, because it is a communist country. According to 2005 statistics, in South Korea, about 46% of citizens follow no particular religion. Protestants account for 18.3%, Catholics 10.9%, and Buddhists 22.8%. In North Korea, around 71.3% of the people claim to be non-religious or atheists.

3 **History** The three kingdoms of Korea (Goguryeo, Silla, and Baekje) were united under Silla in 668. In 918 Wang Geon formed a state called Goryeo. When Mongols invaded China and Korea in the 13th century, the Korean kings survived as Mongol's puppet rulers. In 1392, a general named Yi Seong-gye became a new king of Korea and founded the Joseon dynasty, which lasted until 1910. The Japanese army sent by Toyotomi Hideyoshi invaded Korea in 1592 and again in 1597, but these military expeditions failed.

4 **Korea under Japanese rule** In the 19th century, Joseon leaders closed the country's borders to all nations but China. They recognized the danger of foreign influence, seeing Qing China weakening because of the Opium Wars. So the Koreans followed a cautious policy. To protect the nation, Korea signed a trade treaty with Japan and later with the US. China promoted its trade with Korea in an attempt to block Japanese merchants. Anti-Chinese riots broke out in 1888 and 1889. Japan became Korea's largest trading partner. A rapidly modernizing Meiji Japan defeated China in the First Sino-Japanese War (1894-1895), forcing China to abandon Korea. In 1895, the Japanese were involved in the murder of Empress Myeongseong, who was leaning towards Russia. The Russians were then forced to retreat from Korea. In 1897, Joseon was renamed the Korean Empire, and King Gojong became Emperor Gojong. Japan drove Russia out of Korea completely when Japan defeated Russia in the Russo-Japanese War (1904-1905). In 1905, Japan

placed the Korean Empire under Japanese rule, making it a protectorate. In 1907, Gojong was forced to abdicate his throne and his son Sunjong succeeded him. In 1909, an independence activist An Jung-geun assassinated Ito Hirobumi, who had once been Resident-General of Korea and was a former Japanese prime minister. That gave the Japanese an excuse to annex Korea, which they did in 1910. Japan's rule over Korea lasted until the end of WWII (1910-1945). After Japan was defeated, Soviet troops occupied the northern part of Korea and US troops occupied the southern part. UN-supervised elections were held in the US-occupied south and Syngman Rhee, who was supported by the US, won the presidential election. In the north, Kim Il-Sung, the communist leader, consolidated his position as head of the northern Korea.

5 **Korean War (1950-1953)** In 1950, North Korea invaded South Korea in an attempt to unify the peninsula under its communist rule. This was the start of what is called the Korean War. At first, North Korean forces penetrated deep into South Korea, but the US sent its troops to support South Korea. They pushed North Korean forces back north. In response, China launched a counter-attack and drove the US-backed southern forces back into the south. In 1951, the war's front line stabilized near the 38th parallel, and both sides considered an armistice. They agreed to create a 4-kilometer-wide buffer zone between the two countries, known as the Korean Demilitarized Zone (DMZ). The Korean War ended in 1953, but this was not a truly final end of the war, just an armistice. South Korea has a strict draft system, because Korea is still technically at war and must always be ready to do battle.

Notes

1 the Democratic People's Republic of Korea 朝鮮民主主義人民共和国　the Republic of Korea 大韓民国　despotic 専制的な　side with ～の側につく　annex 併合する　annexation 併合

2 descendant 子孫　Siberia シベリア　Confucianism 儒教　Taoism 道教　prevalent 普及した（形）　atheist 無神論者

3 Goguryeo, Silla, Baekje 高句麗・新羅・百済　Wang Geon 王建（太祖・高麗王）　Goryeo 高麗　puppet ruler 傀儡政権　general 将軍　Yi Seong-gye 李成桂　the Joseon dynasty 朝鮮王朝　expedition 遠征：ここでは日本の朝鮮出兵＝文禄・慶長の役

4 the Opium War アヘン戦争　cautious 注意深い　Empress Myeongseong 明成皇后（閔妃）　lean toward ～に傾く　Gojong 高宗　protectorate 保護領　abdicate 退位する　Sunjong 純宗　An Jung-geun 安重根　assassinate 暗殺する　Resident-General of Korea 韓国統監　supervise 監督する　Syngman Rhee 李承晩　Kim Il-Sung 金日成　consolidate 固める

5 penetrate 侵入する　launch 始める　counter-attack 反撃　stabilize 安定する　armistice 休戦　a buffer zone 緩衝地帯　DMZ 非武装地帯　draft 徴兵　technically 実際・厳密に言うと

【1】次の質問に日本語で答えよ。

1 北朝鮮と南朝鮮（韓国）の違いは何か?

2 北朝鮮での宗教の状態は?

3 三国時代を制して Korea を統一したのはどの国か?

4 1910 年、日本が韓国を併合するきっかけとなった事件とは?

5 1) 朝鮮戦争の発端は何か？そしてその目的は何か。

2) 韓国でまだ徴兵制があるのは何が理由か？

【2】Complete the following timetable in English

668	([1]) united Korea.
918	Wang Geon of Silla formed Goryeo.
13C	Korea surrendered to the ([2]).
1392	Yi Seong-gye founded the Joseon dynasty.
1592,1598	Japan invaded Korea.
1910-1945	Korea was under ([3]) rule.
1945	Korea was divided into two countries, North and South.
1950-1953	Korean War → the formation of the DMZ.

【3】True or False

1) Goguryeo defeated the other two kingdoms, Silla and Baekie, and united Korea in 668. (   )

2) Mongols invaded Korea and killed the king. (   )

3) Yi Seong-gye was a descendant of the Silla dynasty and became the king of Korea. (   )

4) Japan tried to invade Korea twice at the end of the 16th century. (   )

5) During the 19th century, Korea conducted no trade with other countries. (   )

6) Japan annexed Korea, after the assassination of Ito Hirobumi in Korea. (   )

7) The 38th parallel was effectively the border between the North and the South just after the Korean War. (   )

8) The founder of North Korea was Kim Il-Sung. (   )

9) In 1950, the Korean War started with the invasion of the South by North Korean forces. (   )

10) The Korean War ended with an armistice in 1953, establishing the DMZ. (   )

Episode 1 Korea under Japanese rule (1910-1945)

When the Russo-Japanese War ended in 1905, Korea became a protectorate of Japan, and was then annexed by Japan in 1910. The Korean Emperor Gojong was removed from the throne. His son Sunjong became the next emperor. However, the Japanese government finally ended Sunjong's rein and it was the end of the Joseon dynasty. Korea was controlled by Japan from 1910 until Japan's unconditional surrender at the end of WWII.

After its annexation of Korea, Japan suppressed many Korean traditions and customs, aiming at the total assimilation of Koreans into Japanese culture. The Korean language was banned and only Japanese was taught in Korean schools. Koreans were forced to adopt Japanese names, and newspapers were prohibited from publishing in the Korean language. Numerous Korean cultural works and buildings were destroyed or removed to Japan. The Japanese also forced Koreans to worship the Japanese emperor. Nevertheless, some reforms and technologies were promoted under Japanese rule. European-style transportation and communication networks were constructed across the nation. The banking system was consolidated.

Some say that Japanese rule contributed to the modernization of Korea, but some claim that these reforms were carried out for the benefit of the Japanese, not really for Koreans. This has been a controversial discussion topic up to the present day.

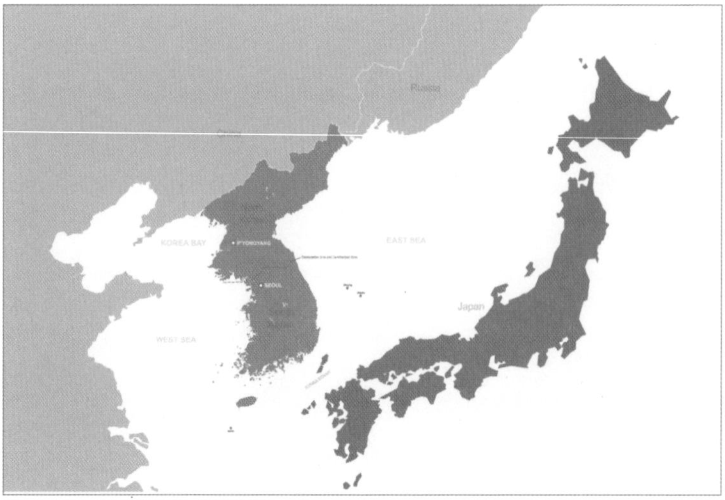

1. Which incident triggered the annexation of Korea by Japan?
   (1) The Anglo-Japanese Alliance
   (2) The Russo-Japanese War
   (3) The Sino-Japanese War
   (4) WWI

2. Japan adopted a policy of assimilating Koreans into Japanese culture. Which following action is NOT mentioned in the reading?
   (1) Japan made Koreans worship the Japanese emperor.
   (2) The Korean people were forced to adopt Japanese names.
   (3) Japanese was taught in Korean schools, but not Korean.
   (4) Korean women were encouraged to marry Japanese men.

3. Which is NOT contribution of Japan to Korea?
   (1) European-style transportation
   (2) protection of Korean cultural works
   (3) European-style communication networks
   (4) consolidation of the banking system

Notes

protectorate 保護領　Gojong 高宗　remove 排除する　throne 王座　Sunjong 純宗　unconditional surrender 無条件降伏　adopt 取り入れる　remove 持ち去る　worship 崇拝する　consolidate 固める　contribute to ～に貢献する　benefit 利益　controversial 議論をよぶ（形）

Episode 2 Soviet Union and the 38th parallel

At the Yalta Conference, Stalin promised to join the Pacific War. On the 8th August 1945, between the dropping of the first atomic bomb on Hiroshima on the 6th and the second bomb on Nagasaki on the 9th, the Soviet Union declared war on Japan. Soviet troops entered Korea immediately. The US government suspected that the Soviet Union would occupy all of Korea. On 10 August 1945, two young American officers—Dean Rusk and Charles Bonesteel—were ordered to draw a clear line that would divide the Korean peninsula permanently. Using a National Geographic map, they decided on the 38th parallel because it would divide the country approximately in half and place the south's capital Seoul under American control. Judging from the extent of US military forces' advancement, the US could have drawn the line further north, but including Seoul and ending the war were more important to America's leaders. The Soviet Union immediately accepted the division.

1. Which statement is true?
   (1) The Soviet Union had not joined the war against Japan before the Yalta Conference.
   (2) The Soviet Union declared war on Japan just before America's use of atomic bombs on Japan.
   (3) The Soviet Union invaded Korea, claiming that the US aimed to take over the country.
   (4) Soviet troops did not invade Korea right away, so that the US wouldn't suspect the Soviet Union's secret plan to rule Korea.

2. Which of these is NOT a reason why the 38th parallel was chosen as the dividing line?
   (1) The Americans thought that the line would divide Korea approximately in half.
   (2) The Americans wanted Seoul to be the capital of South Korea.
   (3) Before the outset of World War II the US and the Soviet Union had already agreed that Korea should be divided at the 38th Parallel.

3. Which statement is NOT true?
   (1) The US was worried that the Soviet Union would occupy the whole of Korea.
   (2) The president of the US ordered two American officials to draw a clear line to divide Korea.
   (3) The Soviet Union hesitated to accept the 38th parallel for a while.
   (4) To keep Seoul was very important for the US.

Notes

Yalta Conference ヤルタ会談　immediately 即座に　approximately およそ　extent 範囲・広がり

Unit
9

Romani

Romani's Great Journey

1. What image do you have of the people long known as "Gypsies"?

2. Why do they want to be called "Romani" today?

3. Originally, where did the Romani come from, Egypt, India, or Spain?

4. The Romani are famous for a certain style of dance. What is it called?

1 **Outline** Have you heard of the "Romani people"? Probably not. How about the "Gypsies"? Most likely yes. Many of us are familiar with the people who have long been called "gypsies." In fact, though, the Romani and gypsies are the same people. But today, we should call them "Rom" or "Romani," not "gypsies," because the latter is not their true name and is an insult to them. The name "gypsies" came from "Egyptians." The Romani were given that name by Europeans who thought that the Romani came from Egypt. But now the Romani want to be called "Rom" or "Romani," which means "man" or "person" in their language. Their original homeland is said to be India, but throughout their history, they have spread all over the world. But we know very little about who the Romani really are.

2 **Different names of the Romani** The Romani have been called by different names around the world. Many Romanis living in France came via Bohemia, the present-day Czech Republic, so they were called "Bohemians." You may know this word is used in a different sense. The word "Bohemian" refers to a person who enjoys a free lifestyle. They are also called "tzigane" in French, "gitano" in Spanish, "zingaro" in Italian, "cigano" in Portuguese and "tigan" in Romanian. "Zigeunerweisen" is a famous work composed by a Spanish composer, Sarasate. This means "Romani music."

3 **Ethnicity, religion, and language** The Romani belong to an Indo-Aryan ethnic group whose origins are in the northern regions of the Indian subcontinent. Their ancestors followed the Hindu religion, but over time, they adopted Christianity or Islam depending on the regions to which they migrated. Muslim Romanis are found in Turkey, Bosnia, Herzegovina, and other places. In countries such as Serbia and Greece, most Romani residents follow the Orthodox religion. In Spain, most Romanis are Roman Catholic. The Romani language is an Indo-Aryan language with roots in Sanskrit. It is spoken by more than two million people. Many Romanis are native speakers of the dominant language in their country of residence.

4 **History** A genomic research report published in 2012 suggests that tribes in northern India, called collectively as the Doma, are most likely the ancestors of modern European Romani. The Romani took two different routes to reach Europe. The first group reached the Balkans in the 12th century, then moved on to southeastern Europe in the 14th century. By the 1440s, they had reached Germany, and by the 16th century, Scotland and Sweden. The second group migrated from Persia through North Africa, reaching the Iberian Peninsula in the 15th century. Ultimately, these two groups met in France. In many of their "host" countries, the Romani were persecuted and excluded from society, with many treated as slaves.

5 **WWII, Holocaust (Porajmos)** The Romani were also the victims of a systematic genocide conducted by Nazi Germany during WWII. This genocide is called “Porajmos.” In 1935, new Nuremberg laws deprived the Romani people in Germany of their citizenship rights, after which the Romani were subjected to violence, imprisonment in concentration camps, and, later, genocide in extermination camps. The policy was also applied by Germany’s allies, notably Croatia, Romania, and Hungary. The exact number of the Romani who were murdered is unknown, but one research estimate reports the total number of victims was between 220,000 and 500,000. Nazi atrocities toward the Jewish people, known as the Holocaust, are well documented and widely known. But few people are aware of the fact that the Nazis killed huge numbers of Romanis and other minority groups.

6 **The current situation** In Europe, Romani people are often associated with poverty and crime, and are sometimes regarded as antisocial outcasts. For this reason, discrimination against the Romani people has continued up to the present day. Amnesty International has reported many instances of anti-Romani discrimination that occurred in the 20th century, particularly in Romania, Serbia, Slovakia, Hungary, Slovenia, and Kosovo. The EU has condemned such discriminatory treatment and is encouraging its member states to ban discrimination against the Romani and to grant them full rights. In 2016, during the International Romani Conference, India’s Minister of External affairs stated that the people of the Romani community were “children of India.” The conference ended with a recommendation that the Romani community, spread across 30 countries, should be recognized as a part of the Indian diaspora.

Notes

1 insult 侮辱
2 Zigeunerweisen チゴイネルワイゼン　Sarasate サラサーテ
3 subcontinent 亜大陸　ancestor 先祖　Sanskrit サンスクリット
4 genomic ゲノムの　collectively まとめて
5 genocide 虐殺　Nuremberg law ニュルンベルグ法　citizenship right 市民権　be subjected to ～を受ける　imprisonment 投獄　concentration camp 収容所　extermination camp（民族）絶滅収容所　ally 味方・同盟国　notably 有名なところでは　victim 犠牲者　atrocity 残虐行為
6 poverty 貧困　antisocial 反社会的　outcast のけ者　India’s Minister of External affairs インド外務大臣　diaspora 離散

【1】次の質問に日本語で答えよ。

1 1)「ジプシー」という呼び方はなぜ今日避けるべきなのか？

2)「ジプシー」とはもともとどういう意味か？

2 ロマニの宗教は？

3 ロマニの移動の二つの流れとは？そしてこの二つの流れはどこで出会ったか？

4 1935 年、the Nuremberg laws でどのようなことが決められたか？

5 2016 年の国際ロマ会議で推奨されたこととは？

Romani estimated percentage of population in European countries (2014)

Bulgaria	10.33%	Hungary	7.05	Moldova	2.49
North Macedonia	9.59	Turkey	5.97	Greece	2.47
Slovakia	9.17	Spain	3.21	Czech Republic	1,96
Romania	8.32	Albania	3.18	Kosovo	1.47
Serbia	8.18	Montenegro	2.95		

【2】Complete the following timetable in English

	Tribes in northern India, called Doma, are possibly the ancestors of modern Romani.
15-16C	The first group of Romani reached the Balkans → Germany → Scotland and Sweden → ([1])
	The second group of Romani reached Persia → North Africa → the Iberian Peninsula → ([2])
WWII	The Porajmos genocide by ([3]) Germany
2016	The International Romani Conference said ([4]) should regard the Romani as a part of the Indian diaspora.

【3】True or False

1) The Romani want to be called "Rom or Romani" not "Gypsies," because they see the latter name as an insult to them. ( )

2) Bohemians, Tsigani and Gitans, Romani, and Gypsies are different names given to the same people. ( )

3) The Spanish composer Sarasate composed "Zigeunerwisen" to commemorate the genocide committed by Nazi Germany. ( )

4) Although the Romani followed the Hindu religion, they accepted other religions in their host countries. ( )

5) The Romani's original language has died out. ( )

6) There were two main migration routes of the Romani to the west. One was through the Balkans, and the other was through north Europe. ( )

7) The Romani were a target of Nazi Germany along with the Jewish people. ( )

8) Hungary, Romania, and Croatia were allies of Nazi Germany during WWII. ( )

9) Today, the Romani people live peacefully around the world. ( )

10) In the Romani conference held in 2016, an Indian minister stated that the Romani are "children of India." ( )

Episode 1 The complicated history of flamenco in Spain

In 2010, UNESCO named flamenco one of the Masterpieces of the Oral and Intangible Heritage of Humanity. When you hear the word “Spain,” you might automatically think of flamenco along with bullfighting. In fact, most of us do think of flamenco as a dance that represents Spain. But some Spanish people have mixed feelings about this connection, because flamenco is generally associated with the Romani. Flamenco is an art form based on various folkloric music traditions of Andalusia in southern Spain. In other words, it is the mixture of cultures that happened to coincide in Andalusia. In Spain, a flamenco performance was once considered a vulgar, even pornographic spectacle, because it was associated with the “gypsy” people. They earned money by performing their dances on the street, in clubs, or in caves. Spanish elites didn’t like foreigners’ association of Spain with the “gypsy” flamenco. But in the 1950s, the Franco regime realized that Spain needed money, because they had been shut out of international trade. This need for money led the Spanish government to promote flamenco as Spanish art form that would attract tourists. Franco increased the number of clubs that specialized in flamenco performances and advertised female flamenco dancers as a tourist attraction. These strategies worked: Spain was able to bring in millions of tourists whose money helped to fund Spain’s economic boom of the 1960s.

1. Some Spanish people have mixed feelings about flamenco dancing, because …
    (1) Flamenco is generally associated with the Romani.
    (2) Flamenco is a dance to represent Spain.
    (3) Spanish people don't want to admit that flamenco originally came from Romanis.
    (4) Flamenco is originally a French dance, but it is now regarded as a Spanish dance.

2. Flamenco has sometimes been considered as vulgar because …
    (1) flamenco dancers were mostly poor street beggars.
    (2) the dances were performed by anti-social people.
    (3) the dances were regarded as somewhat pornographic.
    (4) the words of flamenco songs were impolite.

3. Which is NOT associated with Spain from a tourist point of view?
    (1) bullfighting
    (2) flamenco dancers
    (3) street beggars

4. Why did Franco promote flamenco dances as a tourist attraction?
    (1) He planned to incorporate many peoples' cultures as a way to unite Spain.
    (2) He used the Romani to show that he was tolerant towards all ethnic groups.
    (3) He hoped that the Spanish people would stop discriminating against the Romani.
    (4) He needed money from foreign tourists.

Notes

the Masterpieces of the Oral and Intangible Heritage of Humanity 世界無形文化遺産　bullfighting 闘牛　represent 代表する　folkloric 民族学的・民間伝承の　Andalusia アンダルシア　coincide 偶然出会う　vulgar 下品な　pornographic 扇情的な　spectacle 見せ物　elite エリート　promote 推進する　specialize in ～を専門とする　fund 資金を与える

Episode 2 History of persecution and assimilation of the Romani

Persecution: The Romani people were often used as slaves, which was a common practice in medieval Europe, especially in Romania in the 13th-14th centuries. Some branches of the Romani came as refugees from the Balkans when the Byzantine Empire fell to the Ottoman Empire. Romanis were subjected to persecution, often violence, sometimes even attempts at total ethnic cleansing. In times of social tension, the Romani became scapegoats; for instance, they were accused of bringing the plague at the time of the great epidemic.

Assimilation: During the Habsburg Monarchy under Maria Theresa (1740-1780), the Romani were forced to settle permanently. They were renamed "New Citizens" and had to enter military service. Marriage between Romanis was prohibited. Maria Theresa's successor Josef II banned traditional Romani clothing and the use of the Romani language. In Spain, in 1619, Romanis were forced to assimilate, and the use of the Romani language was prohibited. Romani men and women were sent to separate workhouses and their children sent to orphanages. King Charles III of Spain proclaimed Romanis' equal rights as Spanish citizens and forbade any form of discrimination against them. The use of the word Gitano was also banned. After that, Romanis were referred to as "New Castilians," a name that was also applied to Jews and Muslims.

1. Which statement is NOT true?
   (1) It was common that Romani people were used as slaves in medieval Europe.
   (2) Romani were treated tolerantly in Romania.
   (3) There was a large wave of immigration of Romani after the Ottoman Empire conquered the Balkans.
   (4) At the time of social tension, Romanis sometimes became scapegoats.

2. Which of the following didn't adopt a policy of assimilating the Romani?
   (1) Maria Theresa of the Habsburg Monarchy (2) Elizabeth I of England
   (3) King Charles III of Spain (4) Joseph II of Habsburg Monarchy

Notes

persecution 迫害 assimilation 同化 branch 分派 the Ottoman Empire オスマン帝国 be subjected to ～を受ける tension 緊張 scapegoat 身代わり plague 伝染病 epidemic 疫病の大流行 the Habsburg Monarchy ハプスブルク帝国 Maria Theresa マリア・テレサ successor 後継者 workhouse 救貧院 orphanage 孤児院 forbid-forbade-forbidden 禁止する be applied to ～に適用される

Unit
10
Switzerland
Armed Neutrality

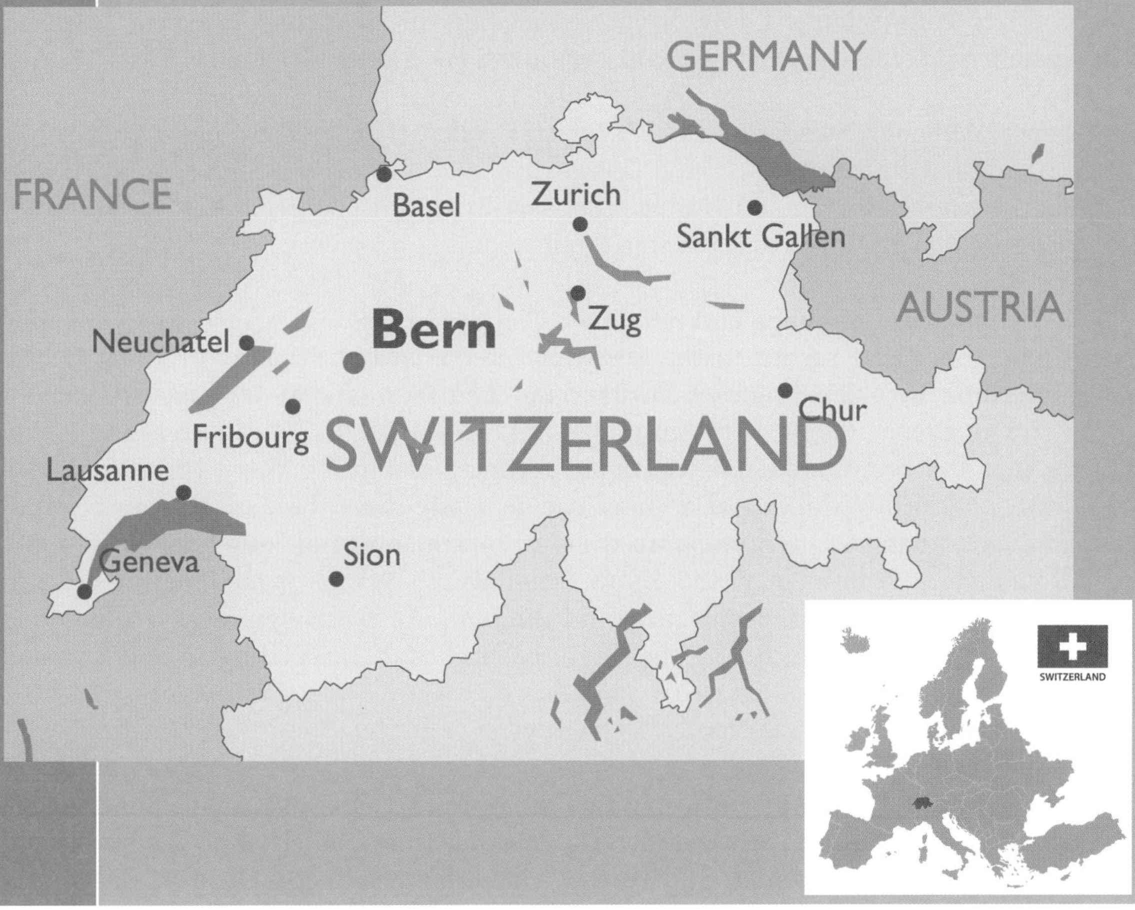

1. What is the capital city of Switzerland?

2. In Switzerland, what name is used for a place equivalent to a "prefecture" in Japan and a "state" in the United States?

3. Switzerland has maintained a unique diplomacy. What is it?

1 **Outline** Switzerland, a landlocked, multilingual European country, is quite unique in its long history of neutrality, that is, in its policy of not getting involved in wars or other conflicts. To hold on to its neutral stance, Switzerland did not join the UN at first, but it finally became a member in 2002. It still avoids, however, membership in such international organizations as the EU and NATO. Thanks to its unique neutral policy, Switzerland has contributed in some ways to world peace. Although Switzerland has a neutral policy, that does not mean that it has no military. In fact, Switzerland is regarded as a militarily strong country. It also has a long history of providing other countries with mercenaries, professional soldiers who are hired to serve in a foreign country's army.

2 **Ethnicity, language and religion** The original Swiss people were probably Celtic tribes that settled in the area and later mixed with many different tribes. According to a 2016 survey, Switzerland has four official languages: German (62.8%), French (22.9%), Italian (8.2%), and Romansh (0.5%). The reason for this is that the country borders Germany, France, and Italy; these three countries have historically influenced Switzerland in many ways. Romansh is an original language that has been recognized as an official national language since 1938. Romansh is a branch of the Latin language that was spoken in the Roman Empire. Many Swiss people are multilingual. As for religion, according to a national survey conducted by the Swiss Federal Statistical Office in 2020, among its 8.5 million people, 33.8% are Catholics, 21.8% are Swiss Protestants, and 5.0% follow other Christian faiths.

3 **History** In the first century BC, the Helvetic Celts came under Roman rule which lasted until the 4th century. During that time, the Helvetic Celts achieved a high level of civilization and traded with their neighbors. Geneva, Basel, and Zurich were linked by military roads, which also linked Rome to the northern tribes. In 800, the country became part of the Frankish Empire, and then, the Holy Roman Empire. Subsequent emperors recognized the importance of this area and granted it some degree of autonomy. In 1291, the rulers of the cantons of Uri, Schwyz, and Unterwalden formed the Swiss Confederation. The Swiss Confederation gained its formal independence from the Holy Roman Empire in 1499. The Swiss Confederation eventually became a union of 13 cantons (now 26 cantons). For centuries, Swiss mercenaries served in other countries' armies. The Swiss Guard of the Catholic Pope is one legacy of this tradition. The Protestant Reformation led to a division between the Protestant followers of Zwingli and Calvin (the German and in some French parts of the country) and the Catholics (the French and Italian parts).

4 **Neutrality** Switzerland is well-known as a neutral country. This might give us the impression that the country is always at peace, but this is not precisely true. To maintain its neutrality, a neutral country needs a military force strong enough to protect itself and must conduct secret diplomacy to avoid conflicts with other

countries. Why did Switzerland choose neutrality? Geographically, Switzerland is located in the center of Europe, and has thus been a strategic target for many countries. For the Swiss, the only way to keep their independence was to stay neutral. Several European powers formally recognized Swiss neutrality in the Treaty of Westphalia in 1648. In 1815, at the Congress of Vienna, Switzerland was given the status of permanent armed neutrality.

5 **WWI and WWII** Switzerland was not invaded during either of the 20th century's world wars. In 1920, Switzerland joined the League of Nations, which was based in Geneva, on condition that it was exempt from any military requirements. During WWII, Switzerland was able to remain independent, serving as a mediator between the Axis and Allied powers. But its strict immigration policies and financial dealings with Nazi Germany caused significant controversy. Switzerland's attitude toward refugees was especially controversial. Over the course of the Second World War, the country admitted as many as 300,000 refugees—but refused many others, including Jews.

6 **Current Situation** In 2002, Switzerland became a full member of the UN. It still remains outside the EU, but is a member of the European Free Trade Agreement (EFTA). It is not likely that Switzerland would join NATO, because NATO is a military alliance. Concerning the Russian invasion of Ukraine, many Swiss people were caught in a dilemma, which raised questions about whether they would be able to protect their permanent neutrality.

Notes

1 landlocked 陸地に囲まれた　neutrality 中立　hold on to ～を守る　mercenary 傭兵

2 Celtic tribes ケルト民族　border ～と国境を接する　Romansh ロマンシュ語

3 Helvetic スイスの　Geneva ジュネーブ　Basel バーゼル　Zurich チューリッヒ　link 繋げる　Frankish Empire フランク帝国　the Holy Empire 神聖ローマ帝国　subsequent 代々の　grant 与える　canton（スイスの）州　Uri ウリ　Schwyz シュヴィーツ　Unterwalden ウンターワルデン（現在は Nitwalden と Obwalden）　the Swiss Confederation スイス連邦　eventually ついには　legacy 遺産

4 diplomacy 外交　strategic 戦略的な

5 the League of Nations 国際連盟　be exempt from ～を免除されている　mediator 仲介者　the Axis power 枢軸国　the Allied power 連合国　controversy 物議　controversial 物議を醸す　admit 受け入れる

6 European Free Trade Agreement 欧州自由貿易連合　military alliance 軍事同盟

【1】次の質問に日本語で答えよ。

1 スイスは中立という政策をとっているが、矛盾する点が2つある。それらは何か？

1.

2.

2 Romansh とはどういう言語か？

3 1) 古代ローマ帝国がスイスに与えた恩恵とは何か？

2) 神聖ローマ帝国はスイスをどのように扱っていたか？

4 中立を保つためには何が必要か？ 2つ答えなさい。

5 スイスはどういう条件で国際連盟に加入したか？

6 スイスと UN および EU の関係について書きなさい。

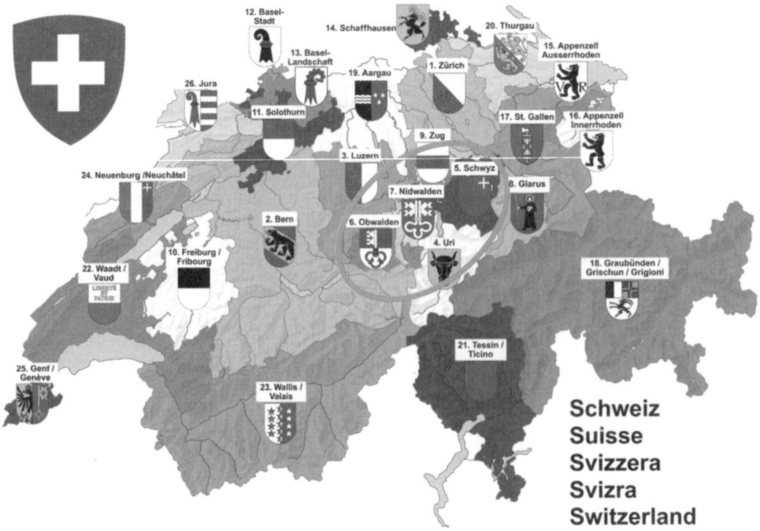

【2】 Complete the following timetable in English

1C.BC-4C.AD	The Helvetic Celts were under Roman rule.
800	The Swiss were ruled by the Frankish Empire.
11C	They came under the rule of the ([1]) Roman empire.
1291	The foundation of Switzerland when Uri, Schwyz and Untervalden signed a charter.
1499	The Swiss Confederation gained independence from the Holy Roman Empire.
1648	The Treaty of ([2]) : European powers formally recognized Swiss neutrality.
1815	Switzerland was given the status of permanent armed ([3]) according to international law.
WWI & WWII	Switzerland remained ([4]).
2002	Switzerland joined the ([5]).

【3】 True or False

1) The ancestors of the Swiss people were Slavic. (   )

2) Thanks to the Roman rule, some important Swiss cities were connected by military roads. (   )

3) Switzerland enjoyed some degree of autonomy under the Frankish Empire. (   )

4) Five Swiss cantons contributed to the foundation of Switzerland in 1291. (   )

5) The Catholic Pope in Rome even now has official Swiss guards. (   )

6) Switzerland has been famous as a neutral country that has no weapons or soldiers. (   )

7) Because of its location, neutrality was the only option available to the Swiss to keep them from being invaded by other countries. (   )

8) In the Treaty of Westphalia, Swiss independence was finally confirmed. (   )

9) Switzerland is now a federal state, protected by the US. (   )

10) Switzerland is now a member of the UN as well as NATO. (   )

Episode 1 Armed neutrality

Armed neutrality is a policy whereby a country vows not to support either side in a war, but to defend itself against attacks from other countries. Sweden and Switzerland adopt a policy of armed neutrality. They have not been caught up in a state of war internationally since 1851. They have pursued active foreign policies and are frequently involved in peace-building processes around the world. Some neutral states such as Dominica and Liechtenstein abandon military power altogether. How about Japan? There has been considerable discussion about the Self Defense Force that Japan maintains. When Japan was defeated in WWII, General MacArthur said that Japan should be "the Switzerland of the Far East." But he soon abandoned this idea because of the rise of communism in China and the Soviet Union and the breakout of the Korean War. The US wanted Japan to serve as an ally against those countries. Now Japan cannot be a neutral state due to the Security Treaty with the United States.

1. Which of the following countries has military power?
   (1) Dominica
   (2) Liechtenstein
   (3) Switzerland

2. General MacArthur wanted Japan to be neutral at first, but he changed his mind. Why?
   (1) He feared that Japan would be an economic and military threat to the US.
   (2) He thought Japan would not be able to stay neutral.
   (3) He thought Japan would join China and Russia in the communist bloc.
   (4) He was concerned about the threat of the communist powers to Asia.

Notes

armed neutrality 武装中立　whereby それによって（関係副詞）　vow 誓う　pursue 追求する　abandon 放棄する　the Self Defense Force 自衛隊　General MacArthur マッカーサー将軍　the Far East 極東　breakout 発生　ally 味方　Security Treaty 安全保障条約

Episode 2　The Nazis and neutrality during WWII

Switzerland managed to maintain its neutrality during WWII, along with Sweden and Portugal. But it has been pointed out that one of the factors that allowed Switzerland to hold on to its neutrality was its trade and dealings with Nazi Germany. The money that Jews deposited in Swiss banks was frozen, the Swiss government refused to accept Jewish refugees, and Swiss banks concealed money that Nazi Germany confiscated from the Jews. Switzerland was severely criticized for such actions. Although many countries declared their neutrality during WWII, only Andorra, Ireland, Portugal, Spain, Sweden, Switzerland, and the Vatican remained neutral to the end. Whether they really remained neutral in every respect is questionable, however. Ireland supplied important secret information to the Allies. Sweden was also involved in intelligence operations with the Allies. Spain allowed Axis ships and submarines to use its ports. Portugal officially stayed neutral, but actively supported the Allies by providing them with overseas naval bases. The US initially remained neutral, but once war broke out in 1939, President Roosevelt persuaded Congress to allow the US to provide military aid to the allies. Vatican City made various diplomatic concessions to the Axis and to the Allied powers alike.

1. Which of the following countries was not neutral during WWII?
   (1) Andorra　(2) Greece　(3) Portugal　(4) Spain

2. Which statement is NOT true?
   (1) Swiss banks concealed money that Nazi Germany had taken from Jews.
   (2) The Swiss government participated in the persecution of the Jewish people.
   (3) The Swiss government did not allow Jewish refugees to enter their country.
   (4) Swiss banks froze the money that Jews had deposited in them.

3. Which statement is NOT true?
   (1) Ireland gave important information to the Allies.
   (2) Sweden was involved in intelligence operations with the Allies.
   (3) Spain helped the Axis by letting them use their ports.
   (4) Portugal supported Nazi Germany by providing them with their naval bases.

Notes

trade 取引　deposit 預ける　freeze 凍結させる　conceal 隠す　confiscate 没収する　the Allies 連合国
intelligence operation 諜報活動　Axis 枢軸国　naval base 海軍基地　concession 譲歩

Episode 3 Swiss banks

Swiss banks quite often appear in crime novels, TV dramas, films, and comic books (Gorgo 13 is an example). Banking in Switzerland dates back to the early 18th century when Switzerland's merchant trade increased. Banking has grown into a complex international business, one of the country's main industries. Swiss banking has a long history of secrecy and client confidentiality. Starting as a way to protect European banking interests, Swiss banking secrecy was codified in 1934 with the passage of a federal law. This law has been used by people and institutions who seek to illegally evade taxes, hide assets, or commit financial crimes. Switzerland has been one of the world's most important overseas financial centers and tax havens since the mid-20th century. The Swiss Bankers Association (SBA) estimated in 2018 that Swiss banks held 25% of all global cross-border assets. Banking in Switzerland has historically played a dominant role in the Swiss economy and society.

1. Swiss banks have been trusted because of …
   (1) low interest rates. (2) their secrecy and client confidentiality.
   (3) polite tellers. (4) pleasant settings.

2. Because Swiss banks are now trusted for their secrecy, they are used as an institution …
   (1) to evade paying taxes. (2) to hide political criminals.
   (3) as a spy. (4) to pay a higher interest rate.

Notes

banking 銀行制度　merchant 商業の　secrecy 秘密性　client 顧客　confidentiality 守秘義務　codify 成文化する　passage 通過　the federal law 連邦法　evade 逃れる　asset 財産　commit（犯罪を）犯す　tax haven 租税回避地　cross-border 国境を超えた　dominant 主要な

Unit 11

Hong Kong

One country, two systems

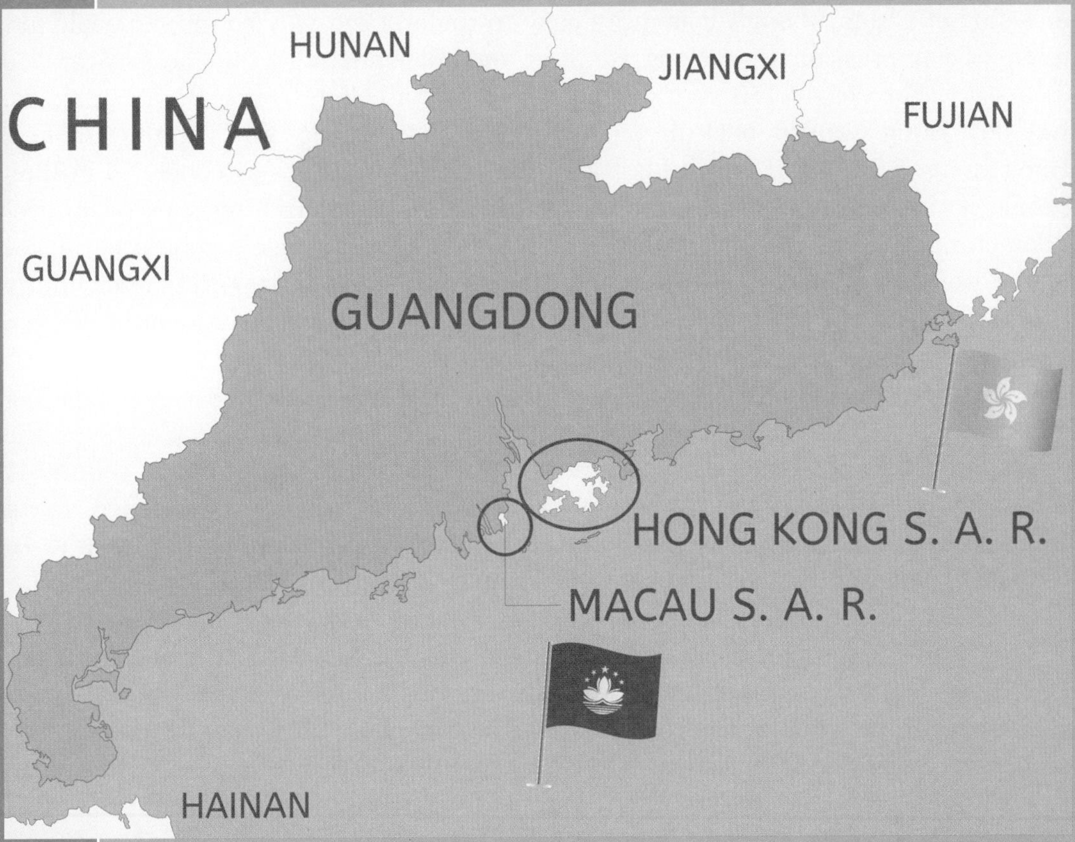

1. Which country owned Hong Kong until 1997?

2. Is Hong Kong now an independent country?

3. Which country owned Macau before 1992?

4. What trade commodity did the British use to conquer China in the 19th century?

1 **Outline** Hong Kong's official name is rather long: The Hong Kong Special Administration Region of the People's Republic of China. Some people might think that Hong Kong and China are separate countries. But not so. Hong Kong is a part of China, though it is quite easy to understand why so many people are under the impression that Hong Kong is an independent state. The answer lies in history. For nearly 150 years, Hong Kong was a colony of the British Empire. But now Hong Kong is back as part of China. As its long official name implies, Hong Kong is a special administrative area of China. There are over 7.5 million people of various nationalities and ethnicities living in Hong Kong's 1,104-square-kilometer area. This makes Hong Kong one of the most densely populated places in the world, with over 6,400 people crammed into each square kilometer. Many residents live in the city's thousands of high-rise, sky-scraper apartment buildings.

2 **History** In the past, Hong Kong was an area of China made up of farming and fishing villages, inhabited by a rather small number of people. Over the centuries, this area gradually became an important port for foreign countries, especially for Western trading nations. When the Qing dynasty weakened, Hong Kong became the target of several western countries which aimed to annex it. In the end, it was the British Empire that conquered China in the First Opium War of 1839-1842. Britain gained Hong Kong as a colony. After the Second Opium War of 1856-1860, Britain further expanded its rule to the nearby Kowloon Peninsula. Finally, in 1898, Britain obtained Hong Kong under a 99-year lease. Under British rule, Hong Kong grew prosperous and became an important global financial and economic center and was returned to China in 1997. China promised to maintain Hong Kong's economic and political systems for 50 years after the transfer. As a special administrative region, under a policy known as "one country, two systems," Hong Kong maintains separate political and economic systems from mainland China.

3 **The current position of Hong Kong** Thanks to British rule in the 20th century, Hong Kong is now one of the world's most significant financial centers and commercial ports. Hong Kong has a unique economic system, characterized by low taxation, minimal governmental market intervention, and an established international financial market. The Hong Kong Stock Exchange is the seventh-largest in the world (2018).

4 **The Umbrella Revolution** According to the agreement with Britain, Hong Kong is guaranteed freedom from Chinese government intervention for fifty years, until 2047. But China has been intervening in Hong Kong's politics. For example, the Chinese government decided that in elections for political executives in Hong Kong, the Chinese government would check the candidates to determine whether they are appropriate or not. Under this law, Hong Kong people cannot freely elect the executives they like. In 2014, protesters against this law resorted to the Umbrella Revolution (the Umbrella Movement), so called because the

demonstrators used umbrellas as a tool for passively resisting and protecting themselves from the Hong Kong police's use of pepper spray against them. The leaders of this Umbrella Revolution were mainly university students.

5 **The Fugitive Offenders Amendment Bill (Hong Kong Extradition Bill)** In 2019, the Hong Kong government tried to pass what was called the Fugitive Offenders Amendment Bill, which would force Hong Kong police to transfer criminal suspects to mainland China. Until then, Hong Kong had been permitted to refuse to transfer criminals to the Chinese government, which allowed the police to protect people who work for Hong Kong's interests. But the Chinese government wanted to arrest the activists against them. Opponents of the bill said it would expose the people of Hong Kong to unfair trials and violent treatment and would give China greater power over Hong Kong. Opponents feared that the law would be used to oppress activists and journalists. Against this bill, a large protest movement grew up, which caught the world's attention. After weeks of demonstrations, the bill was withdrawn. But the leaders of the movement were arrested and imprisoned and since then, the suppression of freedom has continued.

Notes

1 The Hong Kong Special Administrative Region of the People's Republic of China 中華人民共和国香港特別行政区　colony 植民地　administrative 行政上の　densely 密に　populated 人が住んでいる　cram 詰め込む　square kilometer 平方キロメートル　resident 居住者　high-rise 高層の　skyscraper 摩天楼

2 inhabit 居住する　the Qing dynasty 清朝　the First Opium War 第一次アヘン戦争　Kowloon Peninsula 九龍半島　lease 借地権　prosperous 繁栄した　transfer 移譲

3 characterize 特徴づける　taxation 課税　minimal 最小の　intervention 介入　financial 金融の　the Stock Exchange 証券取引所

4 executive 重要人物　candidate 候補者　appropriate 適切な　resort to ～に訴える　the Umbrella Revolution 雨傘革命　passively 消極的に　pepper spray ペッパー・スプレー

5 the Fugitive Offenders Amendment Bill 逃亡犯条例改正案　pass 通過させる　transfer 引き渡す　criminal 犯罪の　suspect 容疑者　arrest 逮捕する　activist 活動家　opponent 反対者　bill 法案　expose A to B　A を B の危険に晒す　trial 裁判　oppress 抑圧する　withdraw 撤回する

【1】次の質問に日本語で答えよ。

1 香港の現在の複雑な位置を決めたのは歴史上のどういう事実か?

2 1) 1842 年、イギリスが香港を得たのはどういう経緯からか？

2) なぜ香港は 1997 年に中国に返還されたのか？

3 香港の経済はどういう特徴を持っているか? 3 つ指摘せよ。

1.

2.

3.

4 2014 年の雨傘運動は何が原因か?

5 2019 年に中国が出した the Fugitive Offenders amendment bill とはどういうものか?

【2】Complete the following timetable in English

1839-1842	The First Opium War → Britain gained Hong Kong from the ([1]　　　　) dynasty.
1856-1860	The Second Opium War → Britain gained ([2]　　　　) Peninsula.
1898	Britain obtained a 99-year lease of Hong Kong.
1997	Hong Kong was returned to China. → “one country, ([3]　　　　) systems”
2014	The ([4]　　　　) Revolution
2019	A big protest movement against the Fugitive Offenders Amendment Bill.

【3】True or False

1) “Hong Kong” has a longer official name. (　)

2) Hong Kong and China seem to be separate countries, but in fact Hong Kong is part of China. (　)

3) In 1898, Hong Kong was leased to Britain for 99 years. (　)

4) Hong Kong was closed to foreign countries for one century under Britain. (　)

5) Since early times, Hong Kong has been an important port for China to trade with foreign countries. (　)

6) Owing to British rule in the 20th century, Hong Kong has been economically behind other parts of China. (　)

7) According to the agreement with Britain, Hong Kong would be able to enjoy political freedom for another one hundred years after Hong Kong was returned to China. (　)

8) The Fugitive Offenders Amendment Bill means that Hong Kong people can’t freely go outside of China. (　)

9) In 2014, there was a large protest movement against the Chinese government called the Umbrella Revolution. (　)

10) With the Fugitive Offenders Amendment Bill, the Chinese government tried to find the Hong Kong people who were working against the Chinese government. (　)

Episode 1 The Opium Wars

In the 19th century, Europeans' demand for Chinese tea, silk, and porcelain became stronger and stronger. But there was not so much demand for European goods on the part of China. This led to a large trade imbalance between China and the European countries. To correct this trade gap, the British started selling large amounts of Indian opium to China. Before long many Chinese people became addicted to opium, which became a major social problem. In 1839, the Qing dynasty leaders ordered that the opium trade should be stopped. In response to this action, Britain attacked China, starting the First Opium War (1839-1842). The Qing leaders surrendered and as a sort of loser's punishment, "presented" Hong Kong to Britain in the 1842 Treaty of Nanking. Under British rule, living and other conditions in Hong Kong quickly improved. During the Taiping Rebellion, which was an attempt to overthrow the Qing dynasty in the 1850s, many Chinese refugees, including wealthy merchants, fled mainland China and settled in Hong Kong. Tensions between Britain and the Qing leaders escalated over the opium trade and finally resulted in the Second Opium War (1856-1860). The Qing government was again defeated and, as a condition of the Convention of Peking, was forced to give up Kowloon Peninsula.

1. Why did the British start to sell Indian opium to China?
   (1) Because the British wanted to start growing opium in China by themselves.
   (2) Although the British wanted many goods from China, they didn't have much to sell.
   (3) Because China couldn't trade with India directly.
   (4) Because Chinese opium was an inferior product.

2. The main result of the First Opium War was …
   (1) victory of the Chinese forces over Britain.
   (2) the collapse of the Qing dynasty.
   (3) the concession of Hong Kong to Britain.
   (4) the participation of Portugal in the war on China's side.
3. The result of the Second Opium War was …
   (1) the victory of the Chinese forces over Britain.
   (2) the concession of Kowloon Peninsula to Britain.
   (3) the intervention of Spain and Portugal into the domestic affairs of China.
   (4) the collapse of the Qing dynasty.

Notes

The Opium War アヘン戦争　porcelain 陶器　imbalance 不均衡　opium アヘン　be addicted to ～の中毒になる　the Treaty of Nanking 南京条約　the Taiping Rebellion 太平天国の乱　overthrow 打倒する　merchant 商人　flee-fled-fled 逃げる　escalate 加速する　the Convention of Peking 北京条約　Kowloon Peninsula 九龍半島

Episode 2 Hong Kong under Britain

By the end of the Second Opium War, Hong Kong had already become an international port thanks to British economic investment. Rapid economic improvement during the 1850s attracted larger and larger foreign investment. Hong Kong further expanded starting in 1898, when Hong Kong became a British colony under a 99-year lease. The University of Hong Kong was established in 1911. Kai Tak Airport was built in 1924. At the start of the Second Sino-Japanese War in 1937, Governor Geoffrey Northcote declared Hong Kong a neutral zone. Hong Kong was occupied by Japan for four years before Britain recovered control of Hong Kong in 1945. The Qing dynasty had already collapsed (1921) and the Chinese Civil War between the Republic of China and the Communist Party of China (1927-1949) followed. Many skilled workers fled to Hong Kong to escape the war. Many more flooded into Hong Kong when the Communist Party won the war in 1949. The British colonial government began reforms to improve infrastructure and public services. Houses were built, the civil service was made less corrupt and more efficient, and public transportation was greatly enhanced. By the early 1990s, Hong Kong had established itself as a global financial center and shipping hub. But then Hong Kong was transferred back to China on 1 July 1997. Under the Joint Declaration, Hong Kong was assured that it would be a "free country" for at least for fifty years. China is violating this Declaration, however, and Britain is now protesting against China's behavior.

1. Under British rule, Hong Kong …
   (1) was given the status of an independent country.
   (2) owned some colonies of its own.
   (3) flourished as an international port.
   (4) wished to become part of China again.

2. Under British rule, Hong Kong achieved all of these EXCEPT …
   (1) the establishment of the University of Hong Kong.
   (2) the construction of an airport.
   (3) economic development.
   (4) the establishment of its own parliament.

3. Which statement is Not true?
   (1) The Qing dynasty ended after WWI.
   (2) The Communist Party won the Civil War.
   (3) When Japan fought against China in 1937, Britain declared neutrality of Hong Kong.
   (4) Many skilled Hong Kong workers fled to Taiwan during the Chinese Civil War.

Notes

investment 投資　lease 貸借権　Kai Tak Airport 景徳空港　(Hong Kong) Governor 香港総督　a neutral zone 中立地帯　the Chinese Civil War 中国内戦　the Republic of China（中華民国 = 台湾）　the Communist Party of China 中国共産党　flood 押し寄せる　infrastructure インフラ・基本的施設　corrupt 腐敗した（形）　enhance 強化する　shipping hub 運送拠点　the Joint Declaration 共同声明　violate 侵す

Episode 3 **Macau**

Macau is also a special administrative region of China. Macau became a Portuguese colony when Ming China ceded it to Portugal in 1557. Macau remained under Portuguese control until 1999, when it was returned to China. Macau was originally a small city, but during Portuguese rule, it became a major resort city and a top destination for gambling tourism. Its gambling industry is larger than that of Las Vegas. Like Hong Kong, Macau's independence is guaranteed for a while after its return to China. It also operates under the policy of "one country, two systems" like Hong Kong. Following the transfer, Macau liberated its casino industry (which previously operated under a government-licensed monopoly) to attract foreign investors. Macau became one of the richest economies in the world on a per capita basis. The people of Macau also have problems with the central government, but they are quieter and less likely to protest than Hong Kong people.

1. Under Portugal, …
   (1) Macau stayed a small city.
   (2) Macau grew into a rich farming area.
   (3) Macau was suppressed by China.
   (4) a gambling tourism industry developed in Macau.

2. Portugal ruled Macau …
   (1) for ten years.
   (2) for 99 years.
   (3) for 100 years.
   (4) for over 400 years.

3. Which statement is true?
   (1) Macau's desire to become independent from China is stronger than that of Hong Kong.
   (2) Macau's casino industry is state-controlled.
   (3) Macau's gambling industry is the second largest in the world after that of Las Vegas.
   (4) It was Portugal that promoted Macau's gambling industry.

Notes

Portuguese ポルトガルの　**Ming China** 明朝　**cede** 割譲する　**destination** 行き先　**liberate** 開放する
operate 運営する　**monopoly** 独占　**investor** 投資家　**on a per capita basis** 一人当たり

Unit

12 The Pope and the Vatican City State

The smallest country in the world

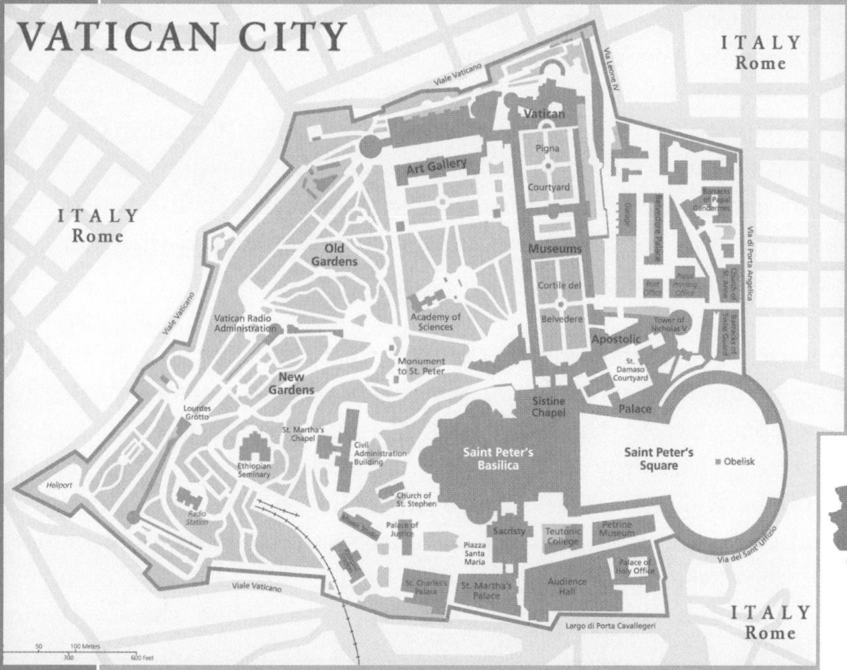

Map of Vatican city in Italy

1. What is the smallest country in the world?

2. Who is the leader of the Vatican?

3. Why is the Vatican City State so rich?

1 **Outline** The Vatican City State is a unique and fascinating place for a variety of historical, religious, and political reasons. It is a fully independent state right in the center of Rome. With an overall area of only 49 hectares and a population of just 800 Catholic church officials, the Vatican City State is the world's smallest country. But the Vatican's small size has never limited its great power and influence on the global stage. That's because the Vatican's head of state is the Pope, the political and symbolic head of the Roman Catholic Church, which boasts 1.3 billion followers worldwide. The Roman Catholic pope is such an important person that a visit by him to any country anywhere in the world is a major, headline-making event, comparable to a state visit made by an American president or the Secretary General of the UN.

2 **History** The Vatican, situated on a hill on the west bank of the Tiber River in Rome, has long been regarded as a sacred place. There was a cemetery on the hill, and St. Peter, supposed to be the successor of Jesus, was killed and buried there. In the 4th century, Emperor Constantine decided to accept Christianity as the only religion of the Roman Empire and built a church over the tomb of St. Peter. The popes gradually exercised political power as well as religious influence. In 395, the Roman Empire was divided into the Western and the Eastern empires. The eastern half became the Byzantine Empire and established the Orthodox Church, with the emperor as the head of the Church. The Pope exercised power in the western Roman Empire and even after the Fall of Western Rome in 476, the Pope survived as a sacred power in Europe. In 800, Charlemagne established the Frankish Empire and approached the pope to ask for his support. Successive rulers asked successive popes to lend the Pope's legitimating power to the rulers. The title "Emperor" was revived in 962, when Otto I was crowned as the successor to Charlemagne. Otto's empire was called the Holy Roman Empire (962-1806), of course, under the Pope's authority. Napoleon dissolved this Empire and again used the authority of the Pope when he declared himself emperor. In short, Europe was formed and continued under the authority of the Pope. The Pope and the rulers of secular nations collaborated throughout most of European history. Sometimes the Pope overwhelmed secular power (for example in the "Walk to Canossa" in 1077), but sometimes he surrendered secular power (the "Avignon Captivity" during 1309-1377).

3 **The "Roman Question" (1861-1929)** For a long time, Italy was a collection of many different city-states. In 1861, Italy was unified and the Kingdom of Italy was founded. This new kingdom annexed Rome and declared it their capital. It was at this time that the Pope was confined to the Vatican. His property was confiscated by the king of Italy. Popes repeatedly claimed their essential independence and demanded the return of their "stolen" property. Between 1861 and 1929, the status of the Pope was called the "Roman Question."

4 **WWII** The independent Vatican City-state came into existence in 1929 through the Lateran Treaty negotiated between the Pope and the government of Italy. The Treaty, signed by Prime Minister Benito Mussolini and Pope Pius XI, established the independent state of Vatican City and reaffirmed the special status of Catholicism in Italy. It is ironic that it was thanks to a fascist power that the Pope recovered his power. The Holy See (the governing body of the Catholic Church) has managed to survive through history, adjusting its level of power with the times. It has been very careful not to get involved in international politics. Today the Holy See has permanent observer status in the UN, although it doesn't have a vote in the UN General Assembly.

5 **How is the Vatican City financed?** There is no taxation system inside the Vatican, because the population of the City is so small. Now that Vatican City cannot get money from taxation, how is it financed? First, it charges tourists admission fees for buildings inside the City. Second, it makes money through stamp and souvenir sales and the sales of its publications. However, the main resource of revenue for the Vatican is contributions from the 1.3 billion Catholics around the world. There are a very large number of Catholic church branches spread all over the world. Those branches support the Vatican financially.

Notes

1 boast ～を誇る　headline-making 見出しを飾る（形）　be comparable to ～に比肩する　the General Secretary of the UN 国連事務総長

2 the Tiber River テベレ川・ティベリス川　sacred 聖なる　cemetery 墓場　tomb 墓　the Orthodox Church 正教会　exercise（権力を）行使する　Charlemagne シャルルマーニ（カール大帝）　the Frankish Empire フランク帝国　successive 歴代の　legitimating 正統な　title 称号　revive 復活する　crown 戴冠させる　the Holy Roman Empire 神聖ローマ帝国　dissolve 解体させる　secular 世俗の　collaborate 協力する　overwhelm 圧倒する　the Walk to Canossa カノッサの屈辱　surrender 降伏する　Avignon Captivity アヴィニョン捕囚

3 city-state 都市国家　confine 閉じ込める　confiscate 没収する　status 状況　the Roman Question ローマ問題

4 reaffirm 再確認する　ironic 皮肉的な　the Holy See 法王庁　with the times 時代に合わせて　observer 立会人・傍観者　the UN General Assembly 国連総会

5 finance 資金を供給する　taxation 課税　admission fee 入場料　souvenir お土産　publication 出版物　revenue 収入　contribution 寄付　branch 支部

【1】次の質問に日本語で答えよ。

1 バチカン市国は世界で最も小さい国であるが、世界に大きな影響力を持っている。なぜか?

2 1) バチカン市国はなぜローマにあるのか？　歴史的起源を説明せよ。

2) 800年にフランク帝国が建国され、それ以降の為政者が教皇に求めたものとは？

3) 教皇と皇帝の力関係は時代によって変わったが、教皇の権威を示した事件と皇帝の力を示した事件をそれぞれ一つずつ挙げなさい。

3 "Roman Question" を説明しなさい。

4 1) 1929年の the Lateran Treaty について説明しなさい。

2) 教皇庁と国連の関係について答えなさい。

5 バチカン市国の収入源で最も重要なものを答えよ。

【2】 Complete the following timetable in English

326	Constantine built a church over the tomb of St.([1]).
476	The Fall of Western Rome
800	The Frankish Empire
962	The Holly Roman Empire
1077	The Walk to ([2])
1309-1377	([3]) Captivity
1861-1929	Roman Question (Pope without property)
1929	The ([4]) Treaty between the Holy See and Italy (Mussolini)

【3】 True or False

1) Rome is the capital city of both Vatican City and Italy. ( )

2) There are about 1.3 million Catholics in the world. ( )

3) The Vatican was founded where Jesus Christ was killed and buried. ( )

4) In the Middle Ages, successive kings and emperors in Europe needed the Pope's authority to back up their power. ( )

5) One example of the Pope's power over secular power was the "Walk to Canossa (1077)." ( )

6) The Pope was forced to live in Avignon during the period 1309-1377. ( )

7) "The Roman Question" is the name given to the conflict concerning the Pope's property and status. ( )

8) The Pope lost his territory from 1861 to 1929. ( )

9) The Vatican City State is now a member of the UN and the EU. ( )

10) The major financial source that supports the Vatican City State is contributions from Catholic followers the world over. ( )

Episode 1 The Pope and fascism

The dispute between the Italian government and the Catholic Church over the territory and the status of the Pope (the Roman Question) ended in 1929 with the Lateran Treaty, which allowed the Vatican to exist as an independent state. Mussolini, the head of the Italian fascist government, signed the treaty on behalf of Italian King Victor Emmanuel III. While the Vatican was officially neutral during WWII, the relationship between the Nazis and the Vatican remains a subject of great controversy. The Catholic Church believes that Catholicism cannot exist under fascism, simply because fascism places the nation above God and also suppresses fundamental human rights. However, Pope Pius XII never did express any direct opposition to fascism. Why? First of all, it was Mussolini who returned the Pope's territory that had been confiscated from him in 1870. Second, the Christian Church had a long history of distrust towards Jews. Third, the Pope thought that Nazi Germany might become the protector of Christianity against rising communism, which denies the existence and practice of any religion. Finally, people simply feared fascists' violence against the Christian Church.

1. Which statement is NOT a reason why the Pope did not protest strongly against fascism?
   (1) He hoped that Mussolini would expand the Pope's territory.
   (2) The Christian Church had long distrusted and disliked Jews.
   (3) The Pope didn't want Nazi Germany to attack the Christian Church.
   (4) Fascism could be used against communism.

2. Which of these statements is the reason given for why Catholicism can't exist under fascism?
   (1) Because in fascism, the nation is more important than anything else.
   (2) Because in fascism, the nation is equal to God in importance.
   (3) Because fascists think fundamental human rights and God are important.
   (4) Because fascists think the nation and God should cooperate.

3. Communism was a stronger threat than fascism to Catholicism, because …
   (1) under communism, the political leader has power over the religious leader.
   (2) communism denies any religion.
   (3) fascism denies equality, but communism denies nationalism.
   (4) communism is more violent than fascism.

Notes

dispute 争い　on behalf of ～に代わって　a subject of controversy 論議のまと　suppress 抑圧する
confiscate 没収する　distrust 不信

Episode 2 The Swiss Guard

It may sound a little odd that the Swiss Guard has been protecting the Pope since 1506. In that year Pope Julius II hired Swiss mercenary forces for his personal protection. At the time, hiring Swiss soldiers as body guards was common among many European kings. Today, the Swiss Guard's role in Vatican City is restricted to protecting the personal safety of the Pope and the city's citizens. The Italian Armed Forces are in charge of the military defense of Vatican City. Recruitment of Swiss Guards is arranged by a special agreement between the Holy See and Switzerland. All recruits must be Catholic, unmarried males, with Swiss citizenship, and with certificates of good conduct. They must be between the ages of 19 and 30 and at least 174cm in height. The armed forces of the Vatican were disbanded in 1970, and Vatican City is now protected by the Hague Convention for the Protection of Cultural Property. This means that the Vatican is protected by international treaty.

1. The Swiss Guard's role in Vatican City is …
    (1) to protect the safety of citizens in Rome.
    (2) to protect the safety of the Pope and citizens in the city.
    (3) to fight against the enemies of the city.
    (4) to do anything the Pope requests.

2. Which statement is NOT true?
    (1) The Swiss Guard fights against any force that threatens Vatican City.
    (2) Vatican City is protected by Italian forces.
    (3) Vatican City is protected by the Hague Convention.
    (4) Vatican City has no armed forces of its own.

3. Which of the following is NOT necessary for candidates of the Swiss Guard?
    (1) being Catholic
    (2) having Vatican citizenship
    (3) being at least 174cm tall
    (4) being unmarried

Notes

mercenary 傭兵　odd 奇妙な　recruitment 新兵募集　recruit 新兵　conduct 行い　disband 解散する
the Hague Convention for the Protection of Cultural Property 文化財保護に関するハーグ条約

Episode 3 Conclave

The election of the Pope takes place in the Sistine Chapel, in a meeting called a "conclave." This is so called because the electors are theoretically locked in "cum clave" (meaning "with key"), until they elect a new Pope. In the election process, the results of each ballot are announced to the world in a unique way. Once the ballots are counted, they are bound and burned in a special stove. The smoke is visible from Saint Peter's Square where a large crowd has gathered. The ballots from an unsuccessful vote are burned with a substance that creates black smoke. When a vote is successful, the ballots are burned alone, sending out white smoke. This white smoke announces to the world that a new Pope has been chosen. The name of the new Pope is announced from a balcony above St. Peter's Square.

1. "conclave" originally means …
   (1) fairness
   (2) with key
   (3) election
   (4) without doubt

2. What is a principle regarding "conclave"?
   (1) The election should be held in the open air.
   (2) The results of the election should be announced to the world.
   (3) The process of the election should be secret.
   (4) The election should be observed by the third party.

3. When a new Pope is decided, …
   (1) people can see black smoke.
   (2) people can see white smoke.
   (3) no smoke appears.
   (4) the new Pope appears on a balcony over St. Peter's Square.

Notes

conclave コンクラーベ（教皇選出会議）　the Sistine Chapel システナ礼拝堂　elector 選挙人　theoretically 理論的には　ballot 投票　bind-bound-bound まとめて縛る　stove ストーブ　visible 目に見える　Saint Peter's Square サン・ピエトロ広場

Unit

13

Kurds

A stateless people

1. Who are the Kurds? Do they have their own country?

2. In which country do the majority of the world's Kurds live?

3. What is their religion?

4. In 2022, Turkey opposed Finland's and Sweden's joining NATO. Why?

1 **Outline** You may know a lot about "Jews" and "Palestinians." But how about the "Kurds"? Probably not so much. They are not so familiar, but they are one of the world's largest ethnic groups who are without their own country. There are some 30 to 45 million Kurds in the world, most of whom are dispersed around the Middle East. For many centuries, the Kurdish people inhabited a part of the Ottoman Empire, called Kurdistan. In those days, the Kurds lived among other ethnic groups relatively peacefully. After the Ottoman Empire ended in 1922, many peoples living within it gained their independence. But for a variety of reasons, the Kurds were unable to do so. The Empire's collapse meant that Kurdistan was conquered by many different countries. Kurdistan is now the name of a region, divided and occupied by Turkey, Iran, Iraq, Syria and Armenia. Over the years, conflicts between the Kurds and their "hosts" have become increasingly frequent and fierce. As a result, the Kurds' desire to have a country of their own has grown stronger and stronger. Several international organizations, including the UN, condemn the Kurds' host countries for their unfair and often brutal treatment of the Kurds.

2 **Ethnicity, language and religion** Kurds (or the Kurdish people) are an Iranian ethnic group, native to a mountainous region of Western Asia called Kurdistan, which means, simply, "Land of the Kurds." Kurds speak "Kurdish," a language that belongs to a west Iranian language related to Persian and Pashto. The majority of Kurds are followers of the Sunni branch of Islam, although there are also many who follow the Shiite branch. Today, 18-20% of the Middle East's Kurds live in Turkey, 15-20% in Iraq, 10% in Iran, and 9% in Syria. Many others live around the world.

3 **History** The name "Kurd" can be traced back to the time of their conversion to Islam in the 7th century. Their reputation for superb military skills made them competent mercenaries in many countries. In the 12th century, the sultan Saladin fought fiercely against the invading Crusader forces, enhancing the reputation of the Kurds as brave soldiers. In the early 16th century, the Ottoman Empire, founded in Anatolia by Sunni Turks, began expanding eastward to fight against the Shiite Safavid Empire in Persia. The Kurds, being Sunni Muslims, willingly followed the Ottomans.

4 **The origin of recent conflicts** When the Ottoman Empire came to an end after WWI, Lebanon, Syria, Iraq, and Kuwait became independent nations. But not the Kurds. An agreement called the Treaty of Sevres (1920) promised to make Kurdistan autonomous, but this promise was not carried out. Another treaty, the Treaty of Lausanne enacted in 1923, made no mention of Kurdistan. Thus, the Kurds' dream of becoming independent was lost. The recent history of the Kurds is a long list of genocides, rebellions, and abuses of all kinds.

5 **Kurds in Turkey** Under the Ottoman Empire, the Kurds were able to live in peace, because the Empire was made up of many peoples who were allowed to maintain their own lifestyle. But, after the Empire collapsed in 1923, Kemal Ataturk established the Turkish Republic. This was an autonomous nation-state, and the Turkish people began demanding a state of a single ethnic identity. They deprived Kurds of their Kurdish identity and called them "Mountain Turks." The Turkish leaders banned the Kurdish language and their traditional dress and suppressed Kurdish political protests in the eastern provinces. Since the 1970s, the European Court of Human Rights has condemned the Turkish government for its human rights abuses. In 1978, the Kurdistan Workers' Party (PKK), a Marxist organization, was formed, whose aim is to gain independence for Kurdistan.

6 **Kurds in Iran** Kurds are also under strong assimilation pressure in Iran and have suffered brutal religious persecution by Iran's Shiite Muslim majority. After WWII, the Soviet Union backed the establishment of an independent country of Kurds in northwestern Iran, but the plan collapsed, after the Soviets' withdrawal in 1946.

7 **Kurds in Iraq** In the late 1970s, Iraq's Ba'ath Party encouraged Iraqi Arabs to settle in the areas where Kurdish majorities lived, particularly around the oil-rich city of Kirkuk. Their aim was to expel Kurds from those regions. The Iraqi government suspected that Kurds were aiding Iranian forces during the Iran-Iraq War of 1980-88. In 1988, the Iraqis used chemical weapons on Kurdish civilians, killing as many as 5,000 Kurds with mustard gas and nerve agents. With the help of the US, many Kurds were evacuated and able to establish a "safe haven" in Iraq.

Notes

1 be dispersed 散らばっている　host 受入国　condemn 非難する　brutal 残虐な
2 Pashto パシュトーン語　Sunni branch イスラム・スンニ派　Shiite branch イスラム・シーア派
3 be traced back to 〜に遡る　conversion 改宗　reputation 評判　superb 素晴らしい　competent 優秀な・能力のある　mercenary 傭兵　sultan スルタン　Saladin サラディン　Crusade 十字軍　enhance 高める　Safavid Empire サファビー朝
4 the Treaty of Sevres セーブル条約　autonomous 自治の　the Treaty of Lausanne ローザンヌ条約　genocide 虐殺　rebellion 反乱　abuse 虐待
5 Kemal Ataturk ケマル・アタテユルク　nation-state 民族国家　Marxist マルクス主義の
6 assimilation 同化　persecution 迫害　back 支持する
7 expel 追い出す　suspect 疑う　aid 助ける　mustard gas マスタード・ガス　nerve agent 神経ガス　evacuate 避難させる　safe-haven 避難所

【1】次の質問に日本語で答えよ。

1 Kurdistanを分割している国を5つ挙げなさい。

2 クルド人の宗教は？

3 クルド人はどういう能力で有名であったか？

4 第一次大戦後、セーブル条約とローザンヌ条約ではクルド人問題はどう扱われたか？

5 1) クルド人がオスマン帝国内では平和に過ごせたのはなぜか？

2) 1923年にトルコ共和国が建国されてからトルコのクルド人の扱いが酷くなったがなぜか？

6 クルド人とイラン人は共にイスラム教徒であるが、その宗派の違いを答えよ。

7 1988年、イラク人がクルド人に対して使った武器とは？

【2】Complete the following timetable in English

7C	Kurds converted to ([1]).
12C	Saladin fought against the ([2]) forces.
16C	Kurds became part of the ([3]) Empire.
WWI	The Ottoman Empire came to an end. → Kemal Ataturk founded the Turkish Republic.
1970s	([4])'s Ba'th Party encouraged Iraqi Arabs to settle in Kirkuk, where many Kurds lived.
1980-88	The Iran-Iraq War

【3】True or False

1) Kurds, Jews, and Palestinians are equally well known as ethnic groups who do not have their own state. (　)

2) Kurdistan is the area where Kurds have lived for many centuries. (　)

3) The Ottoman Empire aimed to be a state of one ethnic identity and treated the Kurds with violence and brutality. (　)

4) Many peoples gained their independence when the Ottoman Empire collapsed. (　)

5) Kurds have been persecuted in their host countries. (　)

6) Kurds have Slavic ethnicity and most of them are Orthodox Christians. (　)

7) Kurds worked as professional, hired foreign soldiers in many countries. (　)

8) The autonomy of Kurdistan was promised in both the Treaty of Sevres and the Treaty of Lausanne. (　)

9) With their independence denied, Kurds resorted to protests and acts of terrorism, and established PKK. (　)

10) Iraq's Ba'ath Party encouraged Kurds to move to Kirkuk because Iraq needed more workers. (　)

Episode 1 Turkey's opposition to Finland and Sweden joining NATO in 2022

Finland and Sweden remained neutral during the Cold War. The two Scandinavian countries were careful not to become involved in any conflicts or to join any defense alliances. But when Russia invaded Ukraine in 2022, they recognized that they would be helpless if Russia were to invade their territories. Therefore, they made up their mind to join NATO. But they encountered a hurdle. Turkey, a NATO member, was reluctant to allow them in. Erdogan, the Turkish president, claimed, "Neither of these countries have a clear, open attitude towards terrorist organizations." He was, of course, referring to the PKK (the Kurdistan Workers' Party), which Turkey regarded as a "terrorist group." PKK is an armed group struggling for the cultural and political rights of the Kurds in Turkey. Many Kurds had fled to Finland and Sweden in the 1970s and 1980s seeking safety. Turkey thought that the Finnish and Swedish governments were protecting those terrorist groups. After some negotiations and some concessions made by Finland, Sweden and NATO, an agreement was reached. At the 2022 Madrid Summit on 28 June, the leaders of Finland, Sweden and Turkey "agreed to a trilateral memorandum." On 5 July 2022, NATO signed for Finland and Sweden to join the alliance.

1. Finland applied for NATO membership along with …
   (1) Denmark.
   (2) Norway.
   (3) Switzerland.
   (4) Sweden.

2. In general, the advantage of being a NATO member is …
   (1) you can join the EU as well.
   (2) you can receive military support if you are attacked.
   (3) you can remain neutral.
   (4) you can also become a member of the UN.

3. Turkey opposed Sweden's and Finland's official participation in NATO, because …
   (1) those two countries have long been enemies of Turkey.
   (2) Turkey feared that Russia would get angry if the two countries joined NATO.
   (3) Turkey thought those two countries were protecting terrorists.
   (4) those two countries remained neutral during the Cold war.

4. PKK is …
   (1) a far-left terrorist group.
   (2) an armed group that works for Turkey.
   (3) an armed group that supports Kurds.
   (4) a terrorist group that supports Ukraine.

Notes

alliance 同盟　encounter 遭遇する　hurdle 障害　negotiation 交渉　concession 譲歩　trilateral 三者の
memorandum 覚書

Episode 2 Saladin

Saladin (1137-1193) is probably the most famous Kurdish person in history. His original name was Yusuf ibn Ayyub. Born into a Kurdish Sunni military family in Tikrit in northern Iraq, he later emerged as a subordinate to the Syrian military leader, Nur al-Din. Participating in three campaigns in Egypt (which was then governed by the Shiite Fatimid dynasty), Saladin became head of the Syrian military force in 1169. In 1171, Saladin and his troops conquered the Fatimid dynasty. He became the Muslim sultan of Egypt, Syria, Yemen, and Palestine, and founded the Ayyubid dynasty. In battles against the Christian Crusaders, he achieved his greatest success with the capture of Jerusalem in 1187. In the Third Crusade, he fought against the English king Richard I (Richard the Lionheart) and made a truce with him. He is a hero in the Arab world, but he is also popular in Europe, because of the generosity he showed to Christians in the Crusades.

1. Which statement is NOT true?
   (1) Saladin was born into a family that followed the Shiite branch of Islam.
   (2) Saladin served as a subordinate to the Syrian military leader, Nur al-Din.
   (3) Saladin took part in military campaigns into Egypt.
   (4) Saladin is popular in Europe because of his generosity towards Christian Crusaders.

2. In the wars against the Christian Crusaders, Saladin …
   (1) captured Jerusalem.
   (2) invaded Iraq.
   (3) established the Fatimid dynasty.
   (4) killed the English King Richard I.

3. Saladin founded …
   (1) the Fatimid dynasty.
   (2) the Ayyubid dynasty.
   (3) the Safavid dynasty.
   (4) the Mamluk Dynasty.

Notes

Yusuf ibn Ayyub ユースフ・ブン・アイユーブ　subordinate 従者　Nur al-Din ヌールッディーン
campaign 戦役　the Shiite Fatimid dynasty シーア派ファーティマ朝　Ayyubid dynasty アイユーブ朝
capture 占領　Lionheart 獅子心王　truce 休戦　generosity 寛容さ

Unit

14

Uyghurs

How can Muslims survive in China?

1. Why are Uyghurs persecuted by the Chinese government?

2. What is their religion?

3. Are Uyghurs ethnically Chinese or Turkic?

4. What's the biggest Muslim minority people living in China?

1 **Outline** Xinjiang is a region located in the far northwestern part of China. Xinjiang is not officially a province of China, but it is an "autonomous region," home to many Uyghurs. The Uyghurs are not Chinese. They are originally a Turkic people who have long lived in Xinjiang. Almost 11 million Uyghurs live in the region, which accounts for just under half of the Uyghurs' total population. Xinjiang includes former Eastern Turkistan, which is thought to be the homeland of the Uyghurs. It is also home to the Kazakhs, the Kyrgyz, and the Chinese-speaking Hui. All are Muslims. This area has been dominated by many different civilizations, including the Chinese, Mongols, Tibetans, and Turks. In the 10th century, the Uyghurs gradually began converting to Islam, and by the 16th century, most had become Muslims. The Uyghurs have long been struggling to achieve their independence from China, but the Chinese government is now treating them brutally, which has caught the attention of the world.

2 **Ethnicity, language and religion** The Uyghurs are a Turkic ethnic group with roots in Central and East Asia. They see themselves as native to the Xinjiang Uyghur Autonomous region (formerly Eastern Turkistan), although the Chinese government denies it. The Uyghurs are one of China's 55 recognized ethnic minorities. Their language is close to Uzbek and Turkish. According to a 2010 survey, the population distribution based on religious affiliation in the region is: 58% Muslim, 32% Buddhist, 9% Taoist, and 1% Christian. The majority of the Uyghur Muslims follow the Sunni branch of Islam of the Hanafi School. A minority of Uyghurs are Shiite Muslims who live in the higher mountainous areas of Tajik and Tian Shan.

3 **History** The Uyghur people have lived in eastern Turkistan ever since the great migration of the Turkic peoples from the Mongolian steppes in the 6th century. By the 11th century, Islam had become the area's dominant religion. In 1759, the forces of China's Qing dynasty expanded into Inner and Central Asia, where they soon established military and bureaucratic organizations and began to call the region Xinjiang, or "the new frontier." The Qing dynasty governed the area through the local Turkic-speaking Muslim elite. From the beginning, there was resistance against this invasion. Eastern Turkestan was formally incorporated into the Chinese Empire as the province of Xinjiang in 1884. In 1949, Mao Zedong formed the People's Republic of China (PRC). The PRC soon created the Xinjiang Uyghur Autonomous region, similar to how it has handled Tibet and Inner Mongolia.

4 **Struggle for independence** Following the break up of the Soviet Union in 1991, many Turkic peoples who had been living in Soviet socialist "colonies" in Central Asia formed independent and autonomous states such as Uzbekistan, Kazakhstan, and Kyrgyzstan. The Uyghurs also expected to be granted independence by the People's Republic of China, but that simply did not happen. Uyghurs' disappointment and frustration led to the rise of a resistance movement

inside Xinjiang, Kazakhstan, and Pakistan. The Chinese government, seeing the resistance and protests in Xinjiang as a serious threat, launched a “Strike Hard” campaign against the movement. Anyone that shows sympathies for independence could be arrested and imprisoned without trial. Since 1914, the Uyghurs have suffered under the cruel pressure by Chinese government.

5 **The current situation** Since 2014, Beijing has been imposing severe suppressive measures one after another on the Uyghurs. More than one million Uyghurs have been arrested and detained in internment camps. The government’s anti-Uyghur actions have included forced labor, suppression of religious practices, and political brainwashing and indoctrination. There have been rumors that the government has even tried to block reproduction—to prevent Uyghurs from producing more children. Chinese authorities have consistently denied all reports of such brutal treatment. They call the internment camps “re-education camps,” whose only aim is to teach “correct” Chinese Communist Party ideology. The UN and other international organizations have severely condemned China’s actions, which have been described as ethnocide and cultural genocide. Some foreign apparel companies, including some Japanese manufactures, were criticized for their use of cotton products made from Uyghurs’ forced labor.

Notes

1 Xinjiang 新疆 province 州 autonomous region 自治区 account for ～を占める Eastern Turkistan 東トルキスタン Hui 回族 dominate 支配する brutally 酷く

2 distribution 分布 affiliation 所属 Taoist 道教信者 Hanafi school ハナフィ学派 Tian Shan 天山

3 steppe 草原 Inner Asia 内陸アジア bureaucratic 官僚の incorporate 組み入れる Mao Zedong 毛沢東

4 Uzbekistan ウズベキスタン Kazakhstan カザフスタン Kyrgyzstan キルギスタン frustration 欲求不満 ‘Strike Hard’ campaign 暴力的テロ猛撃キャンペーン imprison 投獄する trial 裁判

5 detain 拘留する internment camp 収容所 brainwashing 洗脳 indoctrination 教化 apparel 服飾の

【1】次の質問に日本語で答えよ。

1 新疆は中国でどういう政治形態で存在しているか?

2 1) ウイグル人はどの民族に属するか？また彼らの宗教は？

2) ウイグル人の居住権についてウイグル側と中国側の主張の違いは？

3 1759 年に東トルキスタンは清朝中国に支配されるようになったが、中国はこの地域をどのように統治したか?

4 1991 年、ソ連が崩壊した際、中央アジアにいた多くのトルコ民族が独立国家となったが、どのような国が独立を勝ち取ったか?

5 2017 年以来、多くのウイグル人が収容所に送られているが、その目的は何か?

【2】 Complete the following timetable in English

6C	The great migration of the Turkic people from the ([1]) steppes. → Uyghurs settled in eastern Turkistan.
By 11C	Uyghurs had accepted ([2]).
1759	Uyghurs came under the ([3]) dynasty.
1884	Eastern Turkistan was incorporated into the Chinese Empire as the province of ([4]).
1949	The People's Republic of China (PRC) was formed and they created the Xinjiang Uyghur Autonomous Region.
2014	The Chinese government started severe control over Uyghurs.
now	The ([5]) criticizes China's harsh treatment of Uyghurs.

【3】 True or False

1) Xinjiang is formally recognized as a province of China. ( )

2) Uyghurs are originally Chinese, but the Chinese government doesn't admit that. ( )

3) The Uyghurs think Xinjiang, known as Eastern Turkistan, is their homeland. ( )

4) The Uyghurs are a Turkish group and originally came from Eastern Turkistan. ( )

5) Most Uyghurs follow the Shiite branch of Islam. ( )

6) In 1884, Eastern Turkistan formally became a part of China. ( )

7) The Uyghurs gained independence along with other Turkic peoples when the Soviet Union collapsed. ( )

8) In 2014, the Chinese government accelerated their actions to suppress Uyghurs. ( )

9) The Chinese government claims that the purpose of the internment camps is to reeducate Uyghurs. ( )

10) China's actions against the Uyghurs can be regarded as ethno- and cultural genocide. ( )

Episode 1 The Hui – China's preferred Muslims?

45

While the Muslim Uyghurs are being increasingly persecuted in China, the largest Chinese-Muslim minority, the Hui, are being left alone. China's Muslim population now numbers 23 million people, of which just over 10 million are estimated to be Huis, and a little under 10 million are Uyghurs.

Considering that both groups are Muslims, it may seem strange that the Chinese government treat the two groups differently: brutal treatment of the Uyghurs and a tolerant attitude towards the Hui. Why? The reason for the Hui's success has to do with their remarkable assimilation into Chinese society, maintaining their identity over the centuries.

When Mao Zedong founded the People's Republic of China in 1949, he divided the Chinese people into 56 ethnic groups based on language, history, religion, and traditions. Of these groups, ten are Muslim minorities, including the Hui, Uyghur, Kazakh, Dongxiang, Kyrgyz, Salar, Tajik, Uzbek, Bonan and Tatar people. The Hui people are the largest Muslim minority in China, followed by the Uyghurs.

Most of the Hui are descendants of Persian, Arab, and Mongol merchants, handcraftsmen and scholars who came to China between the 7th and the 13th centuries. They survived by intermarrying with the Chinese, which allowed them to be ethnically mixed and to spread across the country. The Hui adopted Mandarin as their mother tongue and changed their Islamic practices to fit Confucianism. In appearance, the Hui are now more similar to the Chinese than they are to Persians or Central Asians. They rarely experience restrictions on their religious freedom and they practice their faith openly.

On the other hand, Uyghurs are ethnically distinct, and do not speak Mandarin as a first language. Most importantly, they have a homeland that they wish to claim for themselves. Many of them seek independence from China. In contrast, the Hui, partly due to their diversity and geographic diaspora, and partly because of their cultural closeness to Chinese, have no political desire for independence.

1. Which of the following statements is NOT true?
   (1) The Hui are Muslims, as are the Uyghurs.
   (2) The Hui are the largest Chinese-Muslim minority.
   (3) The Hui live relatively freely compared to the Uyghurs.
   (4) The population of the Hui is far larger than that of Uyghurs.

2. Why is China's attitude toward the Uyghurs different from that it has toward the Hui?
   (1) The Hui are in favor of communism, while Uighurs are not.
   (2) Hui people have been better assimilated into Chinese society than Uighurs.
   (3) Hui people are originally Chinese, while Uighurs are not.
   (4) Hui people are Buddhists, while Uyghurs are Muslims.

3. The Hui don't desire independence mainly because ...
   (1) they don't want to be involved in more trouble after having been oppressed by the Chinese government for a long time.
   (2) they don't have a homeland that they wish to claim.
   (3) they are allowed to practice trade with middle Eastern countries.
   (4) they are originally Chinese.

Notes

Hui 回族　be left alone 放っておかれる　tolerant 寛容な　assimilation 同化　Mao Zedong 毛沢東　Kazaks カザフ族　Dongxiang ドンシャン族　Kyrgyz キルギス　Salar サラール族　Bonan バオアン族　handcraftsman 職人　intermarry 異なった種族と結婚する　Mandarin 中国語　diversity 多様性　diaspora 離散

Episode 2 The Boycott of the Beijing Olympic Games over the Uyghur issue

For the 2022 Beijing Winter Olympic Games, the US, the UK, and Canada declared a diplomatic boycott, along with India, Australia, Lithuania, Kosovo, Belgium, Denmark and Estonia. Those countries said they would send athletes, but no ministers or officials. The US said the reason for this was China's "human rights abuses and atrocities in Xinjiang." Japan joined this movement later. New Zealand, Austria, Slovenia, Sweden, and the Netherlands said they would not send government representatives, but cited COVID as their reason. France was against the boycott, because they thought that such an event should not be politicized. China chose an Uyghur woman as one of the last two torch runners, which the world press regarded as an attempt to cover up their acts of brutality against Uyghurs.

1. Which of the following countries did NOT join the diplomatic boycott of the 2022 Beijing Olympic Games?
   (1) Kosovo
   (2) France
   (3) Estonia
   (4) Lithuania

2. Under the diplomatic boycott, ...
   (1) ministers could be present, if they were invited.
   (2) athletes were not prohibited to take part in the Games.
   (3) no national flags or national anthems were used.
   (4) athletes were told to refuse medals presented by Chinese authorites.

3. The reason for the 2022 Olympics diplomatic boycott was that ...
   (1) China did not protest against Russia's invasion of Ukraine in 2022.
   (2) China was abusing Uyghurs in Xinjiang.
   (3) western countries were protesting against China's aggressive attitude in foreign affairs.
   (4) some illegal acts were committed in the preparation for the Beijing Olympic Games.

Notes

diplomatic boycott 外交的ボイコット　minister 大臣　abuse 侵害　atrocity 蛮行　Covid コロナ
politicize 政治問題化する　torch runner 聖火ランナー　press 報道機関　brutality 残虐行為

Unit
15 Afghanistan
Al-Qaeda and Taliban

1. Which group was behind the September 11, 2011 terrorist attacks on the World Trade Center in New York City?

2. The 1979 Moscow Olympic Games were boycotted by many western countries. Why?

3. What's the difference between Al-Qaeda and the Taliban?

4. What's the name of the Japanese doctor who worked for the Afghan people and was killed by the Taliban?

1 **Outline** Afghanistan was at the center of the Silk Road trade route for centuries, which gave it an important role in connecting West and East. Its location made it strategically important. The country has been involved in many troubles and ruled by a variety of empires and peoples. In the late 20th century, Soviet forces invaded the country. Then, in 2001, following the terrorist attacks on the World Trade Center in New York City, the United States intervened in Afghanistan in pursuit of the terrorists. As soon as the US withdrew its forces in 2021, the Taliban, a very strict Islamic sect, seized the capital city of Kabul, and now Afghanistan is run by a Taliban government.

2 **Religion, ethnicity, and language of Afghanistan** The original Afghan people are said to be Pashtuns, and they still make up the majority of the Afghan population. The group's native language is Pashto, an Iranian language of the Indo-European language family. Because this area was a crossroads for various cultures before Islam came, many religious art works have been left behind. When Islam arrived on the scene in the mid-7th century, most Afghans became Muslims. It has been estimated that 99.7% of the Afghan people are Muslim, mainly of the Sunni Hanafi school.

3 **History** Bactria, an ancient kingdom, was located in the area around present-day Afghanistan. Bactria was conquered by Achaemenian Persia in the 6th century BC. Then Alexander the Great showed up, defeated Persia in the 3rd century BC, and married a Bactrian princess, Roxane, as a symbol of the fusion of West and East. Later, the Mauryan Empire of India occupied southern Afghanistan, bringing Buddhism along with it. Then the Kushans came. And in the 7th century, the area came under the control of the Iranian Sassanian Empire.

4 **Islamization and the formation of Afghanistan** In the 7th century, Arab Muslims introduced Islam to the Afghan tribes and soon most Afghan people became Muslims. In the 13th century, all of Central Asia fell to the Mongol forces of Genghis Khan. Afghanistan remained in a fragmented state until the 1380s, when the Mongol Empire led by Timur began to rule the area. In 1504 the region fell under the Mughal Empire of northern India. In the 18th century, indigenous Pashtuns (known as the Durrani), took over Afghanistan. In 1747, Ahmad Shah united the Pashtun tribes into a single group and built the Durrani Empire (1747-1823).

5 **Three Anglo-Afghan Wars (the Great Game) (1839-1919)** In the 19th century, Britain came to Afghanistan to defend India from Russia. In the First Anglo-Afghan War (1839-42), the British were repelled. After the Second Anglo-Afghan War (1878-1880), the British held most of Afghanistan. After the Third Anglo-Afghan War (1919), the state was officially granted its independence (1926), and named "Afghanistan." During WWII, Afghanistan remained neutral, but after the war, friction among the Pashtun tribes led to tension with Pakistan, which led

Afghanistan to approach the Soviet Union for help.

6 **Afghan Conflict (1978-1989)** In 1953, the pro-Soviet Afghan General Daoud Khan approached the Soviet Union, and the Soviet leader Khrushchev agreed to help Afghanistan. In 1973, Khan overthrew the last king, Zahir Shah, and established the Republic of Afghanistan. In 1978, the Afghan communist party established the Democratic Republic of Afghanistan. This led to a state of civil war (1979). Pakistan and the US supported the rebels, while the Soviet Union backed the communist government. Finally, in 1979, the Soviet Union invaded Afghanistan to protect the Republic. In 1984, Saudi Islamist Osama bin Laden entered Afghanistan to aid the anti-Soviet rebel fighters. In 1988, he formed al-Qaeda, whose goal was to bring about a pure nation governed by Islam. They also targeted America, hoping to undermine its influence in the middle East. In 1989, a peace treaty was concluded, which guaranteed Afghan independence and the withdrawal of Soviet troops.

7 **Afghanistan War (2001-2021)** The Taliban emerged in 1994 as a movement of students from Islamic schools in Pakistan. They besieged Kabul in 1996 and came to power (the first Taliban government). They destroyed ancient Buddhist statues in Bamiyan. On Sept. 11, 2001, al-Qaeda terrorists highjacked four commercial airplanes and crashed them into the World Trade Center. Osama bin Laden was the group's leader. The US government, claiming that the Taliban were hiding Osama bin Laden, launched airstrikes throughout Afghanistan. The Taliban government collapsed in 2001, and in 2011, US forces found and killed Osama bin Laden in Pakistan. In 2021, the American President, Joe Biden, announced the US's withdrawal from Afghanistan. Almost immediately, the Taliban became active again, and on Aug.15, 2021, took over Kabul and established the second Taliban regime.

Notes

1 strategically 戦略的に　intervene 干渉する　in pursuit of ～を求めて　seize 掌握する
2 Pashtun パシュトゥーン人　crossroad 交差路　Sunni Hanafi school スンニ・ハナフィー派
3 Bactria バクトリア　Achaemenian Persia アケメネス朝ペルシア　Roxane ロクサーヌ　fusion 融合　Kushans クシャン朝　the Iranian Sassanian Empire ササン朝イラン帝国
4 Genghis Khan ジンギス･カン　fragment 分裂させる　Timur ティムール　the Durrani Empire ドゥッラーニー帝国
5 repel 退散させる　friction 軋轢
6 Khrushchev フルシチョフ　overthrow 廃止する　state 状態　rebel 反乱者　undermine 弱める　withdrawal 撤退
7 besiege 占拠する　statue 像　crash 衝突させる　launch 開始する　airstrike 空爆

【1】次の質問に日本語で答えよ。

1 アフガニスタンはこれまでなぜ紛争に巻き込まれてきたか？

2 アフガニスタンの宗教と原住民であり現在でも最大多数民族の名前を答えよ。

3 アレキサンダー大王はなぜバクトリア（Afghanistan にあった古代王国）の王女と結婚したか？

4 アフガニスタンが7世紀にイスラム化したあと、ここを支配した帝国の名前を 2 つ答えよ。

5 19 世紀、イギリスがアフガニスタンをほしかった理由は？

6 Osama bin Laden がアフガニスタンに入った目的は何か？

7 アフガニスタン戦争 (2001-2021) で、アメリカがアフガニスタンを攻撃したのはなぜか？

【2】Complete the following timetable in English

BC 3C	Alexander the Great married a Bactrian Princess.
7C	([1]) was brought to the Afghan by Arab Muslims.
13C	→ Mongol Empire → Mughal Empire.
1839-1919	Afghan Wars (the Great Game) between Afghanistan and ([2]).
1926	"Afghanistan" was established.
1978-1989	The Afghan Conflict between Afghanistan and the Soviet Union
1996	The First ([3]) government
2001-2021	The Afghanistan War between Afghanistan and the ([4]) → collapse of the Taliban government
2021	US forces withdrew from Afghanistan. → the second ([5]) government

【3】True or False

1) Islam was the original religion of the group known as the Afghans. ( )

2) It was the Taliban who destroyed Afghanistan's Buddhist statues in Bamiyan. ( )

3) Al-Qaeda's leader was also Taliban's leader. ( )

4) It was the Soviet Union that invaded Afghanistan in pursuit of Osama bin Laden. ( )

5) Alexander the Great married a Bactorian princess as a symbol of the fusion of the West and the East. ( )

6) It was the Mauryan Empire that brought Buddhism to the Afghans. ( )

7) "Afghanistan" was established after the First Anglo-Afghan War. ( )

8) During WWII, Afghanistan remained neutral. ( )

9) After WWII, Afghanistan looked to the Soviet Union because of tension with Pakistan. ( )

10) The Taliban government was overthrown by the US, but the Taliban party survived the Afghanistan War and came back to power after the US left Afghanistan. ( )

Episode 1 Why did the Americans leave Afghanistan in 2021?

The Taliban recaptured Kabul at the very moment that American forces were starting to withdraw from Afghanistan. It was as if the Taliban had been waiting for this perfect chance. Didn't President Biden expect this to happen? But what made the Americans decide to leave Afghanistan? According to Amit Bansal, there were five reasons. First, their aim had been achieved. They entered Afghanistan to arrest Osama bin Laden, who was the leader of Al-Qaeda and who ordered the terrorist attack against the US (on September 11, 2001). The Taliban was thought to be hiding bin Laden somewhere deep in the Afghanistan mountains. When bin Laden was killed in 2011, the Americans' mission was completed. Second, as China was accelerating its activities in the Asia Pacific, the US decided to focus on China's movements, not Afghanistan. Third, the US thought that the "new" Taliban would be different from the former Taliban. The US assumed the new Talibans were trying to change their image as a terrorist group. Furthermore, the new Taliban was much stronger than the "old" Taliban, and the US did not want to become involved with them. Fourth, the US had spent over three trillion dollars in fighting this war over the previous 20 years. Maintaining a large force in Afghanistan was difficult and expensive. Fifth, during the campaign for the Presidential elections of 2020, Joe Biden promised that the US would withdraw from Afghanistan. The reason was that most Americans thought the Taliban was an internal problem of Afghanistan that their government should handle on its own.

1. Which of the following statements is NOT true?
   (1) The Taliban came back to power just when the US started to withdraw from Afghanistan.
   (2) The original purpose of American forces' being in Afghanistan was to find and arrest Osama bin Laden.
   (3) Osama bin Laden was the leader of the Taliban.
   (4) When Osama bin Laden was killed, the primary goal of the American forces was reached.

2. Which of the following statements is NOT a reason for the American forces' withdrawal from Afghanistan?
   (1) China was becoming a more important issue for American politics.
   (2) The US believed that the new Taliban was different from the old one.
   (3) The US thought the new Taliban would support the US.
   (4) The US had already spent a lot of money on Afghan issues.

3. The top priority of the American government at the time had switched to …
   (1) the Russian invasion of Ukraine.
   (2) the global economic recession.
   (3) the COVID pandemic.
   (4) concerns about China's activities in the East.

Notes

recapture 再び占領する　mission 使命　the Asia Pacific アジア太平洋　trillion 兆　previous それまでの　internal 国内の　handle 統制する

Episode 2　Boycott of the Moscow Olympics (1980)

As a protest against the Soviet invasion of Afghanistan, 66 nations boycotted the 1980 Moscow Olympic Games. Led by the US and President Jimmy Carter, the boycott included Canada, Israel, Japan, China and West Germany, as well as most Islamic nations. Some athletes— those from New Zealand, Portugal, Spain, the UK, France, and others—participated in the games under the Olympic Flag. Just 80 countries took part in the Olympics that year, the fewest number since 1956. Many of these countries followed the US boycott initiative, while others cited economic reasons. In retaliation for this boycott, 14 Eastern Bloc nations, led by the Soviet Union, boycotted the next Olympics Games that were held in Los Angeles.

1. The 1980 Moscow Olympic Games were boycotted by many countries because …
   (1) the US was involved in a war against the Soviet Union.
   (2) the countries were protesting against the oppression of ethnic minorities by the Soviet government.
   (3) the Soviet Union left the United Nations.
   (4) the Soviet Union invaded Afghanistan in 1979.

2. How many countries joined the Soviet Union in boycotting the Los Angeles Olympics?
   (1) 66
   (2) 80
   (3) 14
   (4) 15

3. What happened to the Los Angeles Olympics?
   (1) They were held despite the Soviet Union's boycott.
   (2) They were cancelled.
   (3) Only 80 countries took part.
   (4) In the end, the Soviet Union decided to take part in it.

Notes

initiative 発議・主導権　cite 引き合いに出す・言及する　in retaliation for ～の報復として

References

1. Ukraine
https://en.wikipedia.org/wiki/Ukraine
https://en.wikipedia.org/wiki/Ukrainians
Episode 1: Russian invasion of Ukraine (2022)
https://en.wikipedia.org/wiki/2022_Russian_invasion_of_Ukraine
Episode 2 : Volodymyr Zelenskyy
https://en.wikipedia.org/wiki/Volodymyr_Zelenskyy

2. Ireland
https://en.wikipedia.org/wiki/Timeline_of_Irish_history
https://en.wikipedia.org/wiki/Ireland
https://en.wikipedia.org/wiki/The_Troubles
Episode 1: Reformation: the religious split of England and Ireland
https://en.wikipedia.org/wiki/English_Reformation
Episode 2: Prospect of Scottish independence
https://en.wikipedia.org/wiki/Scottish_independence

3. Brexit
https://en.wikipedia.org/wiki/Brexit
https://en.wikipedia.org/wiki/European_Union
https://en.wikipedia.org/wiki/Causes_of_the_vote_in_favour_of_Brexit
Episode 1: Scotland and Ireland over Brexit
https://en.wikipedia.org/wiki/Proposed_second_Scottish_independence_referendum
https://en.wikipedia.org/wiki/Schengen_Area
Episode 2: Who supported Brexit?
https://en.wikipedia.org/wiki/Brexit

4. The Second Cold War
https://en.wikipedia.org/wiki/Second_Cold_War
https://en.wikipedia.org/wiki/2001_Sino-Russian_T
Episode 1: The Cold War
https://en.wikipedia.org/wiki/Cold_War
Episode 2: The Belt and Road Initiative
https://en.wikipedia.org/wiki/Belt_and_Road_Initiative

5.The Israeli-Palestinian Conflict
https://en.wikipedia.org/wiki/History_of_Palestine
https://en.wikipedia.org/wiki/Origin_of_the_Palestinians
https://en.wikipedia.org/wiki/Palestine_Liberation_Organization
https://en.wikipedia.org/wiki/Israel_and_the_United_Nations
https://en.wikipedia.org/wiki/Palestinians
(https://en.wikipedia.org/wiki/Fatah–Hamas conflict)

6. Rohingya

https://en.wikipedia.org/wiki/Rohingya_people

Episode 1: Aung San Suu Kyi

https://www.bbc.com/news/world-asia-pacific-11685977

https://en.wikipedia.org/wiki/Aung_San_Suu_Kyi

Episode 2: Japan and Rohingya

https://en.wikipedia.org/wiki/Rohingya_people

7. Basques

https://www.thoughtco.com/basque-country-spain-1435525

https://en.wikipedia.org/wiki/History_of_the_Basques

https://en.wikipedia.org/wiki/Basque_language

https://en.wikipedia.org/wiki/Basques

Episode 1: Basque Country and Catalonia

https://www.centreonconstitutionalchange.ac.uk/news-and-opinion/basque-country-and-catalonia-different-paths-recognition

https://en.wikipedia.org/wiki/Catalonia

https://blogs.lse.ac.uk/europpblog/2017/11/06/a-tale-of-changing-destinies-why-the-catalans-are-pushing-for-independence-rather-than-the-basques/

Episode 2: Guernica

https://en.wikipedia.org/wiki/Guernica_(Picasso)

8. Korea

https://en.wikipedia.org/wiki/History_of_Korea

https://en.wikipedia.org/wiki/Korea

Episode 1: Japanese rule

https://en.wikipedia.org/wiki/History_of_Korea

https://en.wikipedia.org/wiki/Korea_under_Japanese_rule

Episode 2: Soviet Union and 38th parallel

https://en.wikipedia.org/wiki/Korean_War#Korea_divided_(1945–1949)

9. Romani

https://en.wikipedia.org/wiki/Romani_people

Episode 1: The Complicated history of flamenco in Spain

https://www.smithsonianmag.com/travel/complicated-history-flamenco-spain-180973398/

Episode 2: History of persecution and assimilation of the Romani

https://en.wikipedia.org/wiki/Romani_people

10. Switzerland

https://simple.wikipedia.org/wiki/Switzerland

https://www.nationsonline.org/oneworld/History/Switzerland-history.htm

https://en.wikipedia.org/wiki/Switzerland

Episode 1: Armed neutrality

https://en.wikipedia.org/wiki/Neutral_country

Episode 2: Collaboration with Nazis and neutrality during the WWII

https://en.wikipedia.org/wiki/Neutral_country#Neutrality_during_World_War_II

Episode 3: Swiss banks

https://en.wikipedia.org/wiki/Banking_in_Switzerland

11. Hong Kong

https://en.wikipedia.org/wiki/2019_Hong_Kong_extradition_bill
https://en.wikipedia.org/wiki/Hong_Kong
https://en.wikipedia.org/wiki/Umbrella_Movement
Episode 1: The Opium Wars
https://en.wikipedia.org/wiki/Opium_Wars
Episode 2: Hong Kong under Britain
https://en.wikipedia.org/wiki/Hong_Kong
Episode 3: Macau
https://en.wikipedia.org/wiki/Macau

12. Pope and the Vatican City State

https://www.vaticancitytours.it/blog/how-many-people-live-in-vatican-city/
https://www.history.com/topics/religion/vatican-city
https://en.wikipedia.org/wiki/Vatican_City
Episode 1: The Pope and fascism
https://en.wikipedia.org/wiki/Pope_Pius_XII
Episode 2: The Swiss Guard
https://en.wikipedia.org/wiki/Swiss_Guard
Episode 3: Conclave
https://en.wikipedia.org/wiki/Pope#Election

14. Uyghurs

https://en.wikipedia.org/wiki/Uyghurs
https://en.wikipedia.org/wiki/Uyghur_genocide
https://en.wikipedia.org/wiki/Uyghurs#Religion
https://www.historytoday.com/archive/behind-times/uighurs%E2%80%99-history-china
https://en.wikipedia.org/wiki/Uyghurs
Episode 1: The Hui– China's preferred Muslims?
https://www.britannica.com/topic/Hui-people
https://www.tripsatasia.com/newsletter-articles/china-muslim-hui-uyghur-people
Episode 2: The Boycott of the Beijing Olympic Games over the Uyghur issue
https://www.bbc.com/news/explainers-59644043

15. Afghanistan

https://www.nationsonline.org/oneworld/History/Afghanistan-history.htm
Episode 1: Why did the American leave Afghanistan in 2021?
https://www.india.com/opinion/five-reasons-for-american-withdrawal-from-afghanistan-taliban-attack-us-troops-4894307 ("Five Reasons for American Withdrawal from Afghanistan2, by Amit Bansal, August 17, 2021)
Episode 2: Boycott of Moscow Olympics (1980)
https://en.wikipedia.org/wiki/1980_Summer_Olympics
https://en.wikipedia.org/wiki/1980_Summer_Olympics_boycott

Exploring the Roots of 15 Current Global Issues [B-963]
国際問題のルーツを探る

1　刷　2024年2月14日

著　者	石谷　由美子　Yumiko Ishitani
発行者	南雲一範　Kazunori Nagumo
発行所	株式会社　南雲堂 〒162-0801　東京都新宿区山吹町361 NAN'UN-DO Publishing Co., Ltd. 361 Yamabuki-cho, Shinjuku-ku, Tokyo 162-0801, Japan 振替口座: 00160-0-46863 TEL: 03-3268-2311（営業部：学校関係） 03-3268-2384（営業部：書店関係） 03-3268-2387（編集部） FAX: 03-3269-2486
編集者	加藤　敦
装　丁	銀月堂
組　版	Office haru
検　印	省　略
コード	ISBN978-4-523-17963-4 C0082

Printed in Japan

E-mail nanundo@post.email.ne.jp
URL https://www.nanun-do.co.jp/